White House Ladies

Also by Webb Garrison

White House Ladies

Fascinating Tales and Colorful Curiosities

Webb Garrison

RUTLEDGE HILL PRESS®
Nashville, Tennessee
A Thomas Nelson Company

Published by Rutledge Hill Press, a Thomas Nelson Company, P.O. Box 141000, Nashville, Tennessee 37214.

Typography by E. T. Lowe, Nashville, Tennessee.

Library of Congress Cataloging-in-Publication Data

Garrison, Webb B.
    White House ladies / Webb Garrison.
       p. cm.
    Includes index.
    ISBN 1-55853-417-2 (pbk.)
    1. Presidents' spouses—United States—Ancedotes. I. Title.
E176.2.G3 1996
973'.09'9—dc21   96-44333
                                                  CIP

Printed in the United States of America

6 7 8 9 — 05 04 03 02 01

Contents

Part 3 ❧ First Lady Firsts

Part 4 ❧ First Lady Challenges and Controversies

Part 5 ❧ First Ladies Betrayed

Part 6 ❧ First Ladies and the White House

Introduction

A majority of the forty-two chief executives of the United States, up to and including Bill Clinton, were accompanied into the official residence by their wives. Bachelor James Buchanan and several widowers had to make do with relatives or close friends who served as hostesses. In all, thirty-seven presidents' wives have been first ladies.

The term *first lady* did not become standard until the time of Lucy Hayes, however. Significantly, it was a pioneer female journalist who pounded it into the everyday vocabulary of the nation. Writing a column called "Woman's Letter from Washington," Mary Clemmer Ames consistently referred to the wife of Rutherford B. Hayes as "the first lady."

Titles applied to presidential mates are as numerous and varied as those given to the mansion in which they lived for a time, although Martha Washington was the only first lady not to live in the White House. The wife of the country's first president was called "lady presidentress," but some who balked at so ponderous a term preferred to address her as "Lady Washington." Julia Tyler was frequently addressed as "madame presidentress," but some outspoken republican purists refused to give any title to the president's wife.

In this book I have tried to refer to the presidential mansion by the name used during the presidency involved. Unfortunately, this cannot be done uniformly in the case of wives, since there was no consensus until journalist Ames coined the title used today.

Many volumes are available that give biographical information on the first ladies, so it would be redundant to do so here. Instead, colorful and unusual tidbits fill the pages of this book.

Although a question-and-answer format is not followed, much of the material in the following chapters lends itself to informal quiz sessions among family members and friends. For an example of the way this technique may be used, see chapter 38 on nicknames and other terms of endearment.

The following chapters have been organized under six headings. The first of these relates several tales about first ladies who played important roles in action-packed events, but not all of these events occurred in the United States. Some of them blazed a wide trail in Europe and Asia.

Prior to Eleanor Roosevelt most first ladies were nonpolitical, and only recently have first wives been involved in their husband's campaign for the presidency. Yet several first ladies of the nineteenth and early twentieth centuries voiced their opinions and acted on them as best they could to influence Washington politicians to either support their husbands or to adopt their causes.

Of course a subject such as that of the first ladies lends itself to an exploration of the category of "firsts." This section tends to explore some first lady firsts with more than just lists, but a chapter of random firsts is included because it will always be popular with readers interested in the first ladies.

Unusual turns of events will always distinguish a person's character, and the first ladies were subjected to numerous fateful moments. This section ranges from tragedy to serendipity to the peculiar and culminates with the several ways in which some first ladies were able to capitalize on their unique status.

Perhaps the most controversial section of this book is that which explores the element of presidential infidelity. It is no small claim to say that, relative to the number of women involved, no other group of American women have been more sexually betrayed. Some early presidents may have had secret relationships that have never been revealed, but the spotlight of media attention focused on the White House and its occupants in this century shows that several first ladies have had less than faithful husbands.

Finally, with the lone exception of Martha Washington, every first lady has had the White House in common with the others. The thirty-six-room residence was unfinished when Abigail and John Adams took up residence in 1800. Abigail dubbed it "the castle"—a name that did not stick—and fumed that no servants were provided at federal expense. It was called the White House at least once in 1811, and the name came into wider use when the burned-out shell was whitewashed after the British torched it during the War of 1812. Yet as late as the Civil War, letters and documents issued in the house then more than sixty years old were invariably marked as coming from the Executive Mansion. Called by whatever name, the residence of forty-two first families has seen goings-on unlike those of any other residence in North America.

While it has been home to the first families, almost every first lady has left her mark on the residence. This last section looks at how they entertained, what pets they allowed, and other ways in which they made a home out of government housing.

The first ladies are as intriguing as their mates who held the nation's highest office, and some of them make their husbands look bland and colorless. A hint of that undefinable spirit is contained in the forty chapters that follow in the tales of some of the most interesting women this country has ever seen.

Part 1

First Ladies of Action

Lou Hoover was the only first lady who mastered the Chinese language—both spoken and written.

1

Lou Hoover

Adventures in China

*I*t's been a hard day, but a good one; the Russian soldiers are in temporary barracks."

"How many are here?"

"About seven hundred, more or less. They have nothing more powerful than a rifle, but from their looks they are seasoned veterans."

"What about your workers? Are they willing to follow orders?"

"Of course!" laughed Herbert Hoover, scheduled soon to celebrate his twenty-sixth birthday. "My experience in the mines is the only reason I am in charge of putting up barricades. Among the thousand or so Chinese who are here with us, not a man would risk his life outside the settlement. They follow my orders and work hard, because they know their safety depends on getting our defenses ready."

Lou Hoover briefly closed her blue eyes and leaned back in her chair. Her day had been devoted to setting up food distribution centers and a temporary hospital. Weary from pedaling her bicycle since early morning, she was too tired to worry about the Boxers.

Her husband, by now "an old China hand" with a wealth of experience gathered during coal-hunting expeditions, watched Lou begin to doze. He was glad she could sleep briefly; tomorrow would be another hard day for everyone in the Tientsin foreign settlement.

They were there, he remembered with a half-smile, because of Lou's sinus trouble. Had it not flared up, they would almost certainly have been in Peking, probably packed into the British legation along with scores of other refugees.

Peking might be relatively safe, but what would two active young Americans do with their time and energy in such a place? Here in Tientsin, they could at least stay busy and feel that they were doing something worthwhile.

Since the small foreign settlement was bounded on one side by a river, barricades were needed on only three sides. There was no sand, so hastily requisitioned sacks were filled with rice or sugar or wheat—whatever was available—before being added to the barriers that were now nearly waist high.

Trouble had been brewing for many months. The influx of foreigners, including mining engineer Hoover, boosted the resolve and the strength of the secret societies pledged to rid the nation of them. Known to the Chinese as *I-ho-ch'uan,* most foreigners understood the name to mean "righteous and harmonious fists," which lent itself to the title "boxers."

When he was hunting gold in Australia in 1898, Hoover knew nothing about the Chinese movement. Sending a cable proposing marriage, he received a prompt acceptance and returned to California for his bride. After a honeymoon of one night, in February 1899 they sailed for China and an exciting opportunity to seek both gold and coal. Herbert expected to do most of the field work. Although his bride was perhaps the only female in America with a geology degree, she was also skilled in making maps and drafting reports.

In preparation for the trip, Lou Henry had gathered as many Chinese-language books as she could find in Monterey. Herbert laughed and solemnly informed her that "not one foreigner in a hundred ever learns more than a few words in a Chinese dialect."

Lou did not argue with her bridegroom. By the time they reached their destination, however, she was beginning to read Chinese with reasonable accuracy. Once she was immersed in the culture of their new home, she rapidly learned to speak the language. Except for a few missionaries, she was the first American woman to master the intricate language.

Lou's knowledge of Chinese proved invaluable when the Boxer Rebellion threatened to engulf the nation in June 1900. From refugees she learned that the Boxers had sworn to rid the land of all foreigners and Chinese Christians. Seeking to revitalize traditional Chinese values that were threatened by the influx of Westerners, the insurgents gained the support of the empress dowager,

Herbert Hoover, the first chief executive born west of the Mississippi River, photographed while receiving an honorary degree.

Tz'u Hsi. Soon many units of the imperial army marched under the flags and emblems of the Boxers.

By now better acquainted with Chinese history, Lou told her husband that she felt she understood the rebellion. "Britain gave these folk a fearful drubbing in the Opium War," she reminded him. "Then they took another beating in their wars with Japan. Their national pride has been mortally offended, so they are out for revenge. When an allied fleet took the forts at Taku on June 16, to the nationalists this was the last straw."

Whether or not her analysis was accurate in all of its details, Lou Hoover was right in identifying the seizure of Taku as crucial. Once it was in foreign hands, the Boxers went on a rampage. In the provinces of Hopei and Shansi they killed nearly every Westerner. By the time they headed for the foreign settlement at Tientsin, corpses were floating down the river in a steady stream.

Hoover's barricades performed well when put to the test, but while the enemies were held at bay, they used their firearms freely. Riding about the settlement to visit the wounded and to feed the hungry, Lou tried to keep her bicycle close to the walls of the houses. She was never hit, but on one occasion a bullet punctured one of her tires.

Shells from the artillery of the Boxers fell around the compound day and night. During a two-hour interval one afternoon the field pieces targeted the house in which the Hoovers were living. An explosion in the back yard was the signal that the barrage had begun. Soon a second projectile passed over the house and landed in the road just in front of it. A third shell came through a window and smashed part of the staircase.

Several newspaper reporters who also lived in the house rushed to see what had happened. One of them, perhaps poet Joaquin Miller who was representing the Hearst chain of papers, was astonished to find Lou at a card table playing solitaire. "It looks as though I can't win," she remarked casually. "Let's go brew a nice pot of tea."

On her daily rounds Lou always carried a .38 Mauser automatic pistol, but she never had to use it. As captain of the guard around a house packed with Americans, she took her turn during the night watches. Having never been on a firing range, Herbert decided to go about his work of defense unarmed. A gun would be a liability to him, he confided to his wife.

In 1900 the world had nothing like a United Nations to mount a peacekeeping mission, but the crisis in China prompted the hasty formation of an international relief expedition. Soldiers and sailors from the United States, Japan, Russia, England, Germany, France, Austria, and Italy came together to relieve the embattled Westerners in China.

They did not reach Peking until August 14, but news that the expedition was en route came much earlier. As a result the siege of Tientsin was lifted, and on July 13 Hoover sent a one-word cable to Lou's father in Monterey: "Safe."

One day after dispatching the cable, Herbert and Lou boarded a German mail boat and headed for England. To their surprise, they were greeted and cheered by crowds of people when they arrived. Not only had they survived the Boxer Rebellion, but, aided by Lou, Herbert's reputation had soared. Not just in London but also in Melbourne and Sydney, he was now called "the Boy Wonder" of mining.

A single coal deposit discovered by Hoover on the property of a Chinese engineering and mining company in Chihli Province was believed to be worth more than eight million pounds. At his insistence, London had invested heavily and expected to reap enormous profits from China's mineral wealth. His previous experience in Australia was now paying off; most of the sites where he suggested mining for gold were proving to be highly profitable.

While Lou and her husband were in London, diplomatic negotiations led to peace in China. As indemnity for the death and destruction wreaked by the Boxers, the empress agreed to pay 450 million Chinese taels to Western nations over a period of thirty-nine years. Of this total, an amount equivalent to twenty-five million dollars was owed to the United States.

During the administration of Theodore Roosevelt, the outstanding balance of about eighteen million dollars was canceled. In return, China promised to spend that sum educating its young people at American universities. Lou, who took great pride in her ability to write and speak Chinese and in her growing collection of Ming dynasty pottery, may have played an influential role in Roosevelt's decision.

Soon after he and Lou left China, the engineer hailed as the boy wonder made his first million dollars from investments in mining operations. Always accompanied by Lou and aided by her, Herbert rapidly added to his wealth. When Lou became first lady in 1929, she and her husband were counted as among the wealthiest of Americans. By then, few Americans remembered the dangerous episode in the life of the first lady during the violent and deadly Boxer Rebellion in northern China just twenty-nine years prior.

2

Lucy Hayes

In Search of a Body

What happened to the paper?"

Pretending not to hear, her cousin continued to busy herself straightening up the bedroom. Accustomed to reading her newspaper in bed, Lucy Hayes rose and walked through the house. When she spied the missing paper of October 20, 1864, she stared in disbelief as she reviewed the front page.

A battle at remote Cedar Creek, Virginia, was the big news of the day. Confederates under Maj. Gen. Jubal Early had staged a surprise attack just before dawn on October 19. Taken by surprise, Union troops made a disorderly retreat before the arrival of their commander, Maj. Gen. Philip Sheridan. With his return to the field, they re-formed, attacked, and claimed a significant victory. The newspaper account was followed by a long list of casualties that included the name of Col. Rutherford B. Hayes of the Third Ohio Volunteer Regiment as among those left dead upon the field.

Lucy, who had often spent time at the headquarters of her husband, knew that his life had been in danger many times. Two years earlier at South Mountain in Maryland he had been severely wounded and lay in the middle of enemy fire before being rescued. Three times he had been endangered when his horse was shot under him. His luck had apparently run out at Cedar Creek.

Later that morning a messenger delivered a dreaded telegram from the U.S. War Department, but to the delight of the recipient, it said that Colonel Hayes had been severely injured in the Virginia fray.

"What on earth did they do with him if he's alive, but badly hurt?" Lucy demanded of the cousin who was serving as her temporary housekeeper. "If he's alive, I can nurse him back to health . . ." Pausing, she added soberly, "If the newspaper is right, I can give him a proper burial. Either way, I must find out for myself."

Traveling by train to Baltimore, Lucy then went to the military base there and secured the use of an ambulance and driver. In less than seventy-two hours after receiving the contradictory reports about her husband, she was in Winchester, Virginia.

Not knowing that the imposing two-story Logan House had served as Sheridan's headquarters, Lucy stopped there to ask about her husband. Unfortunately, no one knew anything of Colonel Hayes. They could only guess that his body might still be lying where he fell.

Following the Valley Turnpike toward Middletown, Virginia, Lucy Hayes frequently encountered bands of blue-clad stragglers. None of them knew anything about her husband; neither did William Dingas, who had returned to his home near the one-mile post that told her she was near her objective.

Skirting a brush-covered hill and slowly moving westward, the colonel's wife reached the scene of the combat late on the fourth day of her odyssey. Although she had seen numerous battlefields, she was not prepared for what she found near the tiny stream around which the fighting had swirled for most of a day.

A few soldiers, busy trying to burn the carcasses of dead horses, were the only uniformed men in sight. Broken wheels, portions of caissons, and fragments of blankets and uniforms littered the ground in profusion. Here and there the toe of a shoe—always without a mate—pointed toward the sullen sky. Long before she had reached the place, Lucy had noticed that the air reeked with the stench of death.

When questioned, only one of the soldiers recognized the colonel's name. "A Secesh bullet took his horse down fairly early, I heard," he observed. "Don't know what happened to him after that." Glad to have an excuse to take a break from his work, he straightened his back, heaved a sigh, and allowed as how she might learn something at the Belle Grove house. "That's better than a mile south of here, on the way to Strasburg," he explained. "Some folk say October the nineteenth ought to go into the record as the battle of Belle Grove, but I don't like that name. Belle Grove is too close to Three-Top Mountain—the place where they say John B. Gordon and his men used their glasses to look over our camp and make plans for their attack."

After a hasty thanks, Lucy followed the soldier's directions and soon came upon the ruins of what had once been a splendid home. Since it was empty and abandoned, she continued west and found that squatters had taken over what was left of Hottle's Mill.

"No, lady," one of them assured her, "we don't know a thing about the battle. Folks say some of the dead are still lying in the brush, but I can't say for certain."

Suddenly feeling compassion toward the stranger who was about to burst into tears, the fellow made a hopeful suggestion. "Turn north," he said, "and you'll likely run into one of the Stickleys. Lots of 'em are farming up at the end of the valley. If Henry can't help you, maybe you'll run into Annie or Daniel."

Unable to find even one Stickley home, Lucy again spent the night in her ambulance. Daylight revealed that she had stopped within sight of the Valley Turnpike, which she had taken from Winchester. Following it, she soon came upon the burned-out foundation of a house that she judged to have been Daniel Stickley's.

As she stared at the wrecked home in despair, a civilian wandered across the turnpike. Explaining that he had worked at Burnt Mills "until it really did get burnt," he volunteered what seemed to be the first useful information she had been given.

"Folks say that lots of prisoners taken by Early's men were sent to Richmond." He then pointed in the general direction of Washington, sixty-five miles to the southeast, and added, "Most of the wounded Yanks went thataway."

"If Rutherford is alive," Lucy reasoned, "he must have been taken somewhere in the vicinity of the capital."

Her driver, who was more than weary of traveling through the backwoods, announced that he would have to turn in his ambulance in a few days. If he failed to do so, there would be hell to pay from his sergeant, even though an officer had authorized the expedition.

On the second day of the journey toward Washington, Lucy was startled to hear muffled artillery fire. Soon she realized that it did not come from another battle; the regularity indicated that the shots constituted a salute of some sort. Later she learned that Gen.

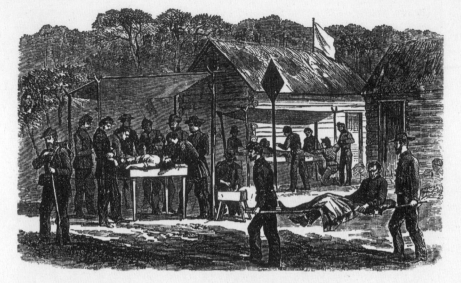

This field hospital in Virginia was probably much less tidy than it appears in this sketch by Edwin Forbes. [HARPER'S HISTORY OF THE CIVIL WAR]

Ulysses S. Grant had ordered a salute of one hundred guns in honor of the victory at Cedar Creek. What's more, Rutherford B. Hayes figured prominently in some dispatches about it, and it was said that his conduct during the battle might merit his promotion to brigadier general.

Hospitals of the capital were already filled to capacity when the wounded from Cedar Creek began to arrive, she learned. As a result, most of them had been shunted into field hospitals just across the Maryland state line.

In the fifth or sixth makeshift shelter for the wounded that Lucy visited, she learned that Colonel Hayes was close by—perhaps at Gibson's Island—hurt too badly to be on his feet, but not considered likely to be added to the death list.

Two weeks after leaving Chillicothe in order to nurse her husband if she found him alive or to bury him decently if she found his body, Lucy Hayes embraced her husband and sobbed wordlessly for many minutes.

When she regained her composure and began firing questions at him, Colonel Hayes gave a wry smile and said that it was not really his fault. Soon after the Rebels had attacked in the predawn fog,

Lucy Hayes loved children and elaborately painted china, although not necessarily in that order.

another of his horses took a direct hit, falling on Hayes's right foot and pinning him in the saddle.

"Now that you've lost four horses," Lucy suggested hopefully, "maybe they won't trust you with another one. You can come home to Chillicothe and hug the little son you've never seen."

Hayes did not get out of uniform as quickly as Lucy hoped. Discharged in June 1865, he resumed his law practice and entered politics, serving three terms as governor of Ohio. In 1876 he campaigned for the presidency, and many audiences heard him tell how "one faithful wife spent two weeks wandering over all Kingdom Come in search of her husband's corpse—only to be surprised by finding him alive and kicking."

Unusual as Lucy's quest had been in 1864, it had little political impact. Hayes appeared to have lost the election in 1876, but politicking in the electoral college was as fierce as the engagement at Cedar Creek some twelve years earlier. At the last minute, northern influence threw the election to the man whose wife spent a week finding him in a tiny makeshift field hospital.

3

Louisa Adams

Bonaparte's Cousin

*I*magine if you can the astonishment your letter caused me. I know not what to do about the selling of the goods [their personal belongings] and I fear I shall be much imposed upon. This is a heavy trial, but I must get through it at all risks. If you receive me with the conviction that I have done my best, I shall be amply rewarded."

Writing from Saint Petersburg in response to a directive penned by John Quincy Adams on December 27, 1814, Louisa Adams had already begun to pack his books. She knew that they were not personal belongings he would want sold, so they were soon shipped to England.

Her task, highly unusual for a married woman soon after the turn of the nineteenth century, was complicated by a language barrier. Louisa was fluent in French, but did not speak or write Russian. After five years in the century-old capital of the empire, her seven-year-old son Charles was at ease in Russian, German, French, and English. Perhaps he could help—at least a little.

Two days after his inauguration in March 1809, President James Madison had set the lives of the Adams family spinning. To the surprise of John Quincy, he was told that he would become the new U.S. minister to Russia. What's more, said the diminutive chief executive, there was no time to weigh alternatives before accepting the post. The Senate had been promised that the nomination would be submitted in just thirty minutes.

Louisa Adams departed Saint Petersburg because her husband was reassigned. [STORM ENGRAVING]

Louisa was bitterly opposed to the move. The education of her two older boys was too important to be interrupted, she insisted. To move meant they must live with their grandparents for an indefinite period, perhaps as long as four years.

Days before the second birthday of their third and youngest son, Charles, the newly appointed diplomat and his family departed New England. Catherine Johnson, a niece whom Louisa had persuaded to go along, would be a great consolation to her. Her husband's nephew, W. S. Smith, had consented to serve as his secretary. Louisa's maid and a black manservant constituted the remaining members of the party.

It took seventy-five days before their vessel nosed its way through ice on the Neva River to reach its destination. Once they were established in the city that Peter the Great had established as his "window on the West," their daily life had little in common with their past experiences.

Louisa found the cost of living unbearably high for her husband's "wretchedly low" salary. In a city filled with the wealthiest of Russians, the diplomat and his family were forced to limit themselves to fourteen servants whom Louisa described as "thieving."

An incessant round of balls and receptions filled their calendar to such an extent that they seldom went to bed before 4:00 A.M.

As a result they altered their schedules and began sleeping until nearly noon. After eating a snack upon arising, they had no real meal until dinner in the late afternoon. Tea was usually served at 9:30 or 10:00 P.M., and supper followed around 1:00 A.M.

Less than a year passed before Louisa began imploring her husband to send her home. That was impossible, John Quincy informed her over and over; they could not afford the expense of the voyage. Louisa had once danced with the czar, but she found that small solace for a rapidly deteriorating relationship with her husband.

Things changed for the better during the too brief spring of 1814. Adams was selected as one of the American commissioners to negotiate the Treaty of Ghent with the British, ending the War of 1812 and addressing the host of issues about which the U.S. and Great Britain had gone to war. Initially seen as requiring several weeks of negotiations, perfection of the treaty dragged on for months. Once it was signed on Christmas Eve 1814, Adams learned that he was to be appointed the American minister to Britain and wrote Louisa directing her to close their Russian home and join him in Paris.

Louisa disposed of their belongings as best she could, meanwhile purchasing a Russian carriage and having it equipped with runners rather than wheels. On her fortieth birthday, February 12, 1815, she and Charles climbed into the vehicle that was packed full of food. Young as he was, the boy understood that they must travel through war-ravaged regions in which it would be difficult to find provisions.

Europe had endured more than a decade of fighting, most of it carried out by the ambitious French general and emperor Napoleon Bonaparte. His downfall began with his invasion of Russia and the epic retreat of the French army from Moscow. These troops had looted and pillaged the countryside as they marched into Russia and again when they returned to France. Some estimates suggested that it might take as many as ten years for the countryside to recover from the Napoleonic Wars.

With the Neva River a solid sheet of ice, it was bitterly cold when Louisa and Charles turned their backs upon the "sterile heartlessness of [their] Russian residence." Paris, more than a thousand miles away, would be a welcome change of climate—geographical as well as political.

While he was in Paris, John Quincy Adams learned that he had been appointed as minister to Britain and wrote his wife directing her to close their Russian home and join him, leaving to her the task of maneuvering through more than a thousand miles of war-torn country.

Within forty-eight hours after beginning her journey, Louisa was perturbed to discover that all of her provisions—Madeira wine included—were frozen solid. Candles were used to melt enough of it for hasty meals, often consumed while the carriage jolted heavily through ruts in ice-covered roads. Whenever her four horses seemed strong enough to endure the pace, she kept going until midnight or later.

Her postillion, Baptiste, lost his way several times and in one village was recognized and denounced as a rogue. Louisa denied personal fear but wrote, "My whole heart was filled with unspeakable terrors for the safety of the child [Charles]."

When conditions made it advisable to replace the runners with wheels, none of the proper size could be bought. They lumbered awkwardly onward, the carriage often tilting dangerously above its too-small wheels. When they reached the Vistula River, the ice was beginning to melt. This made it necessary to hire workers to walk in front of the massive carriage, sounding with poles to test the thickness of the ice.

Once in Prussia, Louisa saw vivid reminders of the destruction that had accompanied Napoleon's passage through the region. Berlin, relatively undamaged by war, was sighted with elation.

Napoleon's triumphant entrance into Paris after escaping the island of Elba in 1815.

Louisa was so travel worn that she decided to spend several days in the city, where she discussed traveling conditions with everyone who spoke French.

It would be well to disguise herself as a military officer, they suggested. Hence Louisa began wearing a large toy soldier hat with a plume that Charles had refused to leave behind. To bolster the impression that her carriage was on a military mission, she strapped her son's toy sword so its hilt was visible through a window. No knowledgeable observer would have given the hat and sword a second glance, since the boy who looked to be no more than fourteen was now serving as courier.

Perhaps deceiving no one except herself, the wife of John Quincy Adams passed through Baden and rolled into Strasbourg. There she learned of Napoleon's escape from exile on the island of Elba and was warned that her newly hired servants could be commandeered from the carriage and impressed into military service.

On the second day after having crossed the French border, the carriage was brought to a sudden halt. Uniformed soldiers—who recognized the coach as being of Russian make—waved their swords and shouted for its occupants to show their heads.

A unit of the imperial guard, hastily reunited to join the former emperor, had only hatred for everything and everyone with Russian ties. In this crisis, Louisa's fluency in French worked wonders. Opening the door of her carriage, she stood upon its step and lauded Napoleon and all the valiant fighting men who were eager to restore him to power.

At this point in the saga of the future first lady's journey through war-torn Europe, accounts differ. According to some, the American diplomat's wife managed to convince the officers of the imperial guard that she was Napoleon's sister. Other reports suggest that she called herself "Bonaparte's cousin, hurrying to embrace him."

Whatever she said to the French veterans, it was the right thing. They parted ranks and permitted her carriage to proceed. Forced by exhaustion to stop a few hours later, Louisa found it impossible to sleep in a hastily improvised bed. The villagers believed that Napoleon was at the gates of Paris with no less than forty thousand men. Recalling that fearful night, Louisa wrote: "This news startled me, but on reflection I thought it best to persevere. I was traveling at great expense, a thing quite unsuited to the paltry salary of an American Minister, and I was sure that if there was any danger Mr. Adams would have come to meet me."

She and Charles rolled into Paris on the evening of March 23, 1815, concluding more than six weeks of hazardous travel. Her heart pounded at the anticipation of joining her husband at the Hôtel du Nord. When she stepped from her carriage shortly before midnight and inquired about her husband, a porter shook his head and told her that Mr. Adams was accustomed to going to the theater regularly and dining afterward with friends.

"If he does not linger too long after the performance ended tonight," said the attendant, "perhaps he will be back at the hotel within an hour or so."

4

Abigail Adams

The Boston Massacre

$\mathscr{I}$ was frightened for you last night."

"So was I. When I started home I thought the whole of Boston was on fire; the clamor was fearful."

By the morning of April 6, 1770, both Abigail and John Adams had a general understanding of what had taken place the previous evening. Neither of them, however, had the slightest idea how it would affect their lives.

Tension between British soldiers and colonials, especially the Sons of Liberty and their adherents, had been rising for months. Sooner or later a clash of some sort was inevitable, Abigail decided after having encouraged her husband to lead the opposition to the Stamp Act. Early in the spring of 1770 the city was rocked by an explosion of anger that triggered the incident soon known as The Boston Massacre.

Before dawn a crude poster was tacked up onto a waterfront post:

> Boston, *March 5,* 1770
> This is to Inform the Rebellious People in Boston that the Soldyers in the 14th and 29th Regiments are determined to Joine together and defend themselves against all who shall Oppose them.
> *Signed,*
> Soldiers of the 14th and 29th

In the light of later developments, Abigail Adams surmised—but never could prove—that the inflammatory notice might have been posted by her husband's cousin, Sam Adams.

The sixteen thousand citizens of the city crawled from bed, shivering; there was a layer of ice on the ground and dark clouds promised snow. A group of adolescent boys spotted a lone British soldier near the custom house and began taunting him before throwing snowballs. Angry, the soldier retaliated by smacking one of the boys so hard that the teenager scurried away, whimpering.

Soon a crowd gathered, and a person never identified yelled, "Let's get the soldier that struck the boy of our barber!"

Calling for help, the soldier tried to make his way to safety in the nearby barracks. There the officer of the day led seven of his men to form a protective barrier between the threatened sentry and the angry mob. Because it was apparent that violence was in the air, Captain Preston directed his men to prime their pieces and load them.

Showered with fragments of ice, pebbles, and snowballs, the soldiers ducked their heads and tried to avoid being hit. According to later testimony, "A tall fellow wearing a bushy white wig and himself wearing a red coat [the color of the hated British uniform]" began taunting the soldiers. "Fire, if you dare!" he cried. "You poor boobs don't even know how to *fire!*"

Since the powerful voice of the large man rose above the din of the crowd, a soldier may have believed his captain had ordered him to fire. Leveling his musket, he directed a shot toward the center of the tumult; one by one, seven of his comrades followed his example. In a matter of seconds, three civilians lay dead in the snow and two others were trying to stop the flow of blood from mortal wounds.

All through that day and far into the night, tumult reigned in the cobblestone streets of Colonial America's third largest city. When the identities of the fallen were made public, fellow workers in the city's rope walk mourned the death of Sam Gray. Few expressed grief that a black dock worker named Crispus Attucks was killed, but the anger of the colonials was widespread.

Seven months pregnant, Abigail Adams held little John Quincy with one hand and her beloved daughter, Abby, age four, with the other. "Don't be frightened, children," she assured them. "Your father is on sentry duty today, and he will take care of you."

Abigail Adams is shown at age twenty-two in this Benjamin Blyth portrait. [MASSACHUSETTS HISTORICAL SOCIETY]

Later that night, when John Adams had returned home, a man named Forester knocked at his door. He explained that he had come on behalf of Captain Preston, who had been arrested for murder. He begged Abigail's husband to join Preston's defense team. Two other men, one of them a cousin of Abigail, had given conditional acceptances that they would fight for the life of the redcoat if John joined them. All observers were unanimous in saying that Preston had not fired upon the crowd; he did not even have his musket in hand.

Both Abigail and her husband knew that a positive response to Preston's plea could mean an end to John's career. An estimated seven thousand Sons of Liberty lived in and around Boston, and many of them had great influence. As he typically did in emergencies, the diminutive attorney turned silently to his wife—one of the best-read and most widely informed women of her day.

Almost as though she had stored it in memory for use on this special occasion, Abigail recited three lines from Shakespeare's *Hamlet:*

> This above all: to thine own self be true,
> And it must follow, as the night the day,
> Thou canst not then be false to any man.

Almost simultaneously she and her husband remembered their visit to Salem, about ten miles from the city, during the previous autumn. That afternoon an awed Abigail had whispered to her husband as they stopped on top of Witch's Hill, "If only the poor women had been able to retain a good lawyer . . ." A good lawyer was what Captain Preston now desperately needed.

Even though she knew that defending a hated redcoat could lead to financial desperation, Abigail encouraged John to put the future of their family in jeopardy. He had the obligation to ensure the defendant received a fair trial and a competent defense.

John Adams agreed, gave Abigail a quick embrace, and headed for his law library. Soon he decided on his strategy. He would invoke English common law, which held that soldiers constituting a lawfully assembled body have the duty—not simply the right—to protect themselves.

Three trials were scheduled: one for Preston alone because he was unarmed, a second for the men under his command, and a third for pro-British civilians said to have fired into the mob from windows of the custom house. Preston was speedily acquitted when a jury was asked to rule on the evidence. Six of Preston's men were found not guilty, and two of them were pronounced to be guilty of manslaughter.

Under English common law, a person on trial could demand "benefit of clergy," meaning that the trial would be conducted before an ecclesiastical rather than a civil court. As soon as Matthew Killroy and Hugh Montgomery were convicted of manslaughter, John Adams called for "benefit of clergy." Automatically granted, it led to the branding of the two soldiers on their thumbs, after which they were released.

The third case, in which civilians were on trial, was resolved quickly. The chief witness against them was found to be guilty of perjury, so he was sentenced to receive twenty-five lashes after having spent a day in the pillory.

Abigail and John believed that the cause of justice had been served. Their joy at the outcome of the legal contest was tempered, however, by the recognition that they had become social outcasts. John was also emotionally and physically exhausted. He seemed despondent and talked about the necessity of writing his will. At age thirty-six, he felt he was nearing the end of his life.

The Braintree (now Quincy) home to which Abigail persuaded her husband to retreat. [U.S. DEPARTMENT OF THE INTERIOR]

"Put your energy to positive use," Abigail insisted. "Instead of sitting down to draw up a will, help me to pack our things so we can leave the city and go home to Braintree. If we act promptly, we can be there in time for spring plowing."

John agreed to leave the city in which he had established his law practice. Soon an entry in his journal revealed how much the change of residence meant:

> April 18 [1771]. Thursday. Fast Day.
> Still, calm, happy Braintree. No journeys to make to Cambridge, no General Court to attend. I divide my time between law and husbandry. Farewell, politics!

After eighteen months in the country, Abigail surprised John by informing him that since he was now fully recovered from his ordeal, she was ready to go back to Boston. When she resumed the life of the wife of an urban attorney, even Abigail did not dream that she would later move far to the south. Twenty-seven years after the Boston Massacre, she and her family took up residence in an unfinished mansion that eventually came to be known as the White House.

5

Anna Harrison

Turnips for Sir Henry

Col. John C. Symmes looked over his assembled officers. "I'm sorry," he began. "We have no orders from General [Anthony] Wayne. I have called you together to get your advice on a different matter—purely personal, but very important.

"Most of you know that for some time I have wanted to take my little daughter to safety at the home of her grandparents. Since it appears that New Jersey is about ready to ratify the Articles of Confederation, I think it is time to move."

"You are right, sir," agreed a burly lieutenant. "But you have not told us what we can do to help."

"I am in urgent need of a powerful horse," their leader explained. "He must be able to carry more than normal weight. In addition to the animal, two very large leather saddlebags are essential and I will have to have at least a bushel of the best turnips that can be bought."

"You plan to take the girl to Long Island, yourself?"

"Correct. I have waited as long as possible, so the time is now urgent."

"That means you will risk your life going through British lines?"

"Of course. I expect to follow the Philadelphia road as far as possible. One of the British uniforms we captured a few weeks ago seems to be just my size."

"If captured when dressed as a redcoat, you will be hanged as a spy. What will happen to the girl then?"

"These are risks I cannot avoid taking," Symmes responded. "General Washington has need of me in the field. I cannot leave little Anna here; the British are on the move again, and this time they may head for Morristown. If they do, everyone in Flatbrook [adjacent to Morristown]—not just my little Anna—will be in danger."

The officers nodded understanding of the plan, and one of them volunteered to lend his big Belgian horse. "Turnips will be easy, this time of year," a captain said. "Oversize saddlebags won't be found readily, but I'll undertake to get them."

Three-quarters of a century later, the former Anna Symmes seemed to have just two great interests in life. She was eager to follow the Civil War exploits of her grandson, Benjamin, as he went from battle to battle. Her second source of pleasure was the telling of girlhood stories to small boys and girls living in the neighborhood.

"My father stuffed me feet first into one of those big saddlebags," she would explain. "I was just four years old and small for my age. He filled the other saddlebag with splendid new-crop turnips, put on the uniform of a redcoat private, and struck out for Long Island."

As the widow of President William Henry Harrison remembered the adventure, her father was challenged at a number of points. When British sentries demanded to know his business and his destination, he pointed to the saddlebag at his right and responded: "I a taking New Jersey turnips to Sir Henry. Here—take a look for yourself, if you like."

No one bothered with more than a casual glance at the turnip-filled bag, so the girl curled up on the left side of the horse was not detected. She and her father entered New York, the second largest city of colonial America, early one morning in July 1779.

Symmes, a New Jersey judge who had volunteered for military service, was appalled at what he saw as they rode into New York. House after house lay in charred ruins from the big fire of September 21, 1776, and the much smaller but still devastating blaze of 1778. Anna's father was not surprised to find the Beekman mansion undamaged. He knew that it had served for a time as the headquarters of Gen. William Howe, whose capture of New York had brought him knighthood, and he assumed that British soldiers had saved it from the fire that destroyed at least five hundred homes.

Many of the soldiers who permitted "a sack of turnips" to pass were Hessian mercenaries.

"Be very still, Anna," her father whispered. "The city is swarming with thousands of redcoats."

Even though they were safely within the city, danger was far from over. To deceive the British, Symmes had to seem to be riding toward the headquarters of the military commander, Sir Henry Clinton. That meant a long detour before he dared to head toward a ferry that would take him to Long Island's village of Southold.

Reaching their destination safely, Anna Tuthill Symmes was consigned to the care of the grandmother for whom she was named. Her father made it safely back to New Jersey and participated in some of the last battles of the American Revolution.

Anna Tuthill, a woman of considerable means, soon persuaded her husband that her small namesake should learn her letters at Clinton Academy in Easthampton. She was still enrolled in the school when the defeated British evacuated New York in November 1783.

Anna's widowed father, whom she had not seen since her ride in one of his saddlebags, came to see the redcoats leave. Sir Guy Carleton, who had succeeded Clinton in command, initially planned to resist to the last man. When he saw that the odds against him were hopeless, he used a small rowboat to reach a British warship anchored far out in the harbor.

With Anna at his side, Colonel Symmes watched as the last boatload of enemy soldiers moved away from the city, then gave a mighty whoop of joy. After a short visit, he returned to New Jersey and resumed his seat on the state supreme court. Soon, however, he began hearing tales of wealth to be had in the West. Without having seen the tract, he bought about five hundred thousand acres of "wild land" not far from the site on which Cincinnati was founded.

After the war, Anna's grandmother sent her to Mrs. Isabella Graham's boarding school on Broadway in New York, where she received the equivalent of today's high school education. At the time she had no idea that she would be the first wife of a U.S. president to be so well educated.

When her widower father decided to take a new bride, he came to Long Island to get her. Anna, now nineteen years of age and called "darkly beautiful," accompanied the newlyweds to their rough-hewn home in North Bend, Ohio.

In 1795 Anna married William Henry Harrison in spite of her father's strenuous objections. Since he had no savings, the soldier and his bride spent their honeymoon days at Fort Washington, where he was stationed. The couple lived happily in Vincennes, Indiana, despite family tragedies in which five of their ten children died.

Harrison resigned from the army in 1798 to become secretary of the Indiana Territory, and the following year he served as the territorial delegate to Congress before being appointed territorial governor in 1800. During his twelve years as governor, he negotiated a number of treaties with the Indian tribes of the northwest, opening up the area for settlement and ending an Indian uprising at the battle of Tippecanoe in 1811. When American forces faltered in the area during the War of 1812, Harrison was made commander of those forces and consolidated the nation's holdings throughout the region. After the war he served in the House of Representatives from 1816 to 1819 and in the Senate from 1825

Anna Harrison had the shortest tenure of any first lady and is the only first lady not to assume any of her official duties.

to 1828. John Quincy Adams appointed Harrison in 1828 as the first U.S. minister to Colombia, but he was recalled the following year by Andrew Jackson.

When she learned that some of her husband's admirers were trying to send him to Washington to become chief executive, Anna Harrison objected violently. "Paw," as she called him, would be subjected to tremendous stress if he should succeed Martin Van Buren in office.

His first campaign for the presidency failed in 1836, but Harrison ran again in 1840 with John Tyler as his running mate. After one of the first media-hyped campaigns in American history, with the catchy slogan of "Tippecanoe and Tyler Too" to enhance themselves with the voters and the fear engendered by the Panic of 1837, the sixty-eight-year-old Harrison was elected president, the oldest man thus far to gain the executive mansion.

Long afterward, neighbors remembered that when Anna Harrison learned that her husband would be president, she wept openly. Reluctant to have anything to do with the nation's highest office, she remained at home to pack their things and was not present at Harrison's inauguration on the bitterly cold, rainy day of March 4, 1841.

During the ceremony Harrison contracted a cold that developed into pneumonia. He died of what doctors then called pleurisy fever on Sunday morning, April 4, thirty days after taking the oath of office, thus serving the shortest term of any U.S. president.

Anna Harrison never assumed the role of mistress of the White House. She was preparing to board a stagecoach for Washington when word arrived that her husband had died. Sympathetic lawmakers in Congress passed legislation providing financial aid to the grieving widow: a cash grant of $25,000 as a lump-sum pension and "the franking privilege," which meant that for the rest of her life she could mail letters without paying for postage.

At the beginning of the Civil War, Anna's grandson, Benjamin, enlisted with the Seventieth Indiana Infantry Regiment. By war's end he had earned the rank of brigadier general. A well-established corporation lawyer after the war, he was elected to the Senate in 1881 and elected president in 1888 by the electoral college, although his opponent—Grover Cleveland—won the popular vote.

Nonetheless, forty-eight years after her husband had become the ninth president of the United States, Anna Harrison's grandson took the oath of office as the nation's twenty-third chief executive. Anna achieved a particular fame with her grandson's inauguration: No other woman has been the wife of one president and the grandmother of another.

At age eighty-eight, when congratulated on her family's achievements, she was prone to say: "Connections with U.S. presidents mean very little to a girl who went into New York in a saddlebag, disguised as a sack of turnips."

6

Martha Washington

Mender of Pantaloons

In December 1777, the sights around his army's winter camp at Valley Forge led George Washington to write:

> To see men without clothes to cover their nakedness, without blankets to lay on, without shoes, by which their marches might be traced by the blood from their feet, and almost as often without provisions as with, marching through frost and snow, and at Christmas taking up their winter quarters within a day's march of the enemy, without a house or hut to cover them till they could be built, and submitting to it without a murmur, is a mark of patience and obedience which in my opinion can scarce be paralleled.

Many of his men died that winter. Valley Forge had not been his first choice for the camp. Initially, his army had been comparatively comfortable at Whitemarsh, a beautiful valley about fourteen miles from Philadelphia, but by the end of the first week of December it was no longer safe when the British occupied the nearby city. So with his half-clad, half-barefoot army he marched to a spot about twenty miles north of Philadelphia.

There was little danger that the British would strike the encampment at Valley Forge. It was too remote and rugged to make an inviting target, even in summer. During the most severe months of winter it could not be reached. An additional advantage of the site

Washington's headquarters at Valley Forge.

was its proximity to York, Pennsylvania, where the Continental Congress was temporarily sitting. If the British moved toward the town, they could be halted—provided Washington's cold and starving troops were able to lift their muskets.

Valley Forge took its name from the fact that it adjoined the winding Schuylkill River and earlier was the site of two or more forges at which blacksmiths worked. It was not a prosperous area, however. In the entire valley there was only one sturdy house, now used as Washington's headquarters. His men either erected crude log huts, dug tiny caves into hillsides, or tried to survive in shelters made of tightly packed snow.

Less than three weeks after moving to the rugged winter camp, Washington noted that almost three thousand of his men were "barefooted and otherwise naked, hence unfit for duty." Some of the most severely frost-bitten soldiers were sent to farmers' cottages, but the majority of the sick and injured remained with their outfits.

Soon after recording the results of his gloomy pre-Christmas assessment, the Continental commander looked up from his desk and saw his wife standing at the door. Martha Custis Washington

Martha Washington made seven trips to her husband's headquarters during the war and endured the hardships of Valley Forge, tending the wounded, mending clothes, and bringing provisions from Mount Vernon. [J. C. BUTTRE ENGRAVING]

had spent much of the previous winter at his headquarters, but she had been warned that a stay at Valley Forge would put her life in danger. Ignoring the advice of military leaders and her friends, Martha made her way from Virginia to Pennsylvania to be with her husband. Barely five feet tall, to Washington she seemed almost to fill the doorway when she appeared unexpectedly.

Born in 1731 at the Chestnut Grove plantation of her parents, Martha Dandridge developed an almost passionate love for horses as a small girl. Her father sometimes joked that she gave all of her love to animals, so had none left for books. That comment stemmed from the fact that her handwriting was barely legible and she never learned to spell correctly.

When it came to what was then called "wifely arts," the situation was different. Martha learned to weave, to sew, and to make jelly and pickles for winter use. When taught the rudiments of knitting, she became permanently interested in this art. Like many other girls then, she mastered embroidery before age ten and designed and executed a sampler that included every letter of the alphabet.

At age seventeen Martha became mistress of her own household when she married Daniel P. Custis, a Virginia planter thirteen years her senior. They had four children, but only two, John Parke and Martha Parke, grew to adulthood. When her husband died in 1757, Martha became one of the richest women in Virginia. Her two homes, thousands of acres, and substantial wealth were the envy of many who knew her.

Col. George Washington of the First Virginia Regiment, colonial militia, became enamored with the lovely young widow soon after meeting her in 1758. For their wedding he wore the dress uniform of his regiment, not knowing that he would spend much of their married life as a soldier.

When made commander in chief of Colonial forces in 1775, Washington headed an army of inexperienced enlistees who were allowed to leave their units after a few months' service. The opposing British force was composed of combat-hardened veterans of many European wars, including mercenaries from the Continent, all led by professional British officers.

In spite of the glaring contrast between British and Colonial armies, Washington managed to drive the Redcoats from Boston. Any elation over that victory was brief, however, for the Colonials soon lost New York City. Timely victories in New Jersey, at Trenton and Princeton, allowed the Colonials to continue the struggle for independence.

The revolutionary cause endured a certain element of chaos on all fronts, not just the battlefield. Washington himself was not above being second-guessed by political and military rivals anxious to take his place. While he succeeded in staying in command of his army, he suffered two significant defeats in 1777 in Pennsylvania, at Brandywine and Germantown, which permitted the British to occupy Philadelphia and drove the Continental army to Valley Forge.

When Martha Washington arrived there, the army could at best place only eight thousand men in the field if called upon to do so. How long these men would remain fit for duty was Washington's greatest question. With the harshest weeks of winter still before them, the mid-December cold was so intense that many tried to sit all night around fires kindled in the fields. When a man could no longer sit, he laid down in a bed of frost and snow covering stony ground.

In addition to the lack of shelter, there was also a lack of food and clothing. There was little that Martha could do to fight hunger, but clothing was a different matter. She could not help every needy man, so she spearheaded an effort to organize women's sewing circles and dedicated herself to helping everyone she met.

The lack of shelter and bitterly cold weather made life miserable for Washington's soldiers at Valley Forge.

During January and February 1778 the skills that Martha had acquired in late childhood were put to constant use. Night after night, after her husband had gone to bed, she sat knitting by the fire. Happy soldiers who received these unexpected wool coverings for their bare feet soon learned the source of their gifts. They frequently visited the commander's headquarters afterward to display some piece of clothing in need of repair and to ask "General Washington's lady" if there were any way something could be done.

There are no records of how many soldiers benefited from Martha's needlework, but the diary of a man identified only as a sergeant from New Jersey contains a story of her willingness to help the soldiers. The sergeant had slipped on the ice and split his trousers. Too embarrassed to approach the wife of his general, he took shelter in a covered bridge not far from Washington's headquarters and sent a friend to the house to ask for Martha's help. Without hesitation, she asked to be led to the sergeant and quickly repaired his trousers. The sergeant reputedly returned to his outfit and insisted on showing his pants to anyone who paused long enough to hear him exclaim, "The general's little wife mended my pantaloons!"

Martha Washington returned to Virginia in the spring of 1778 but spent the next two winters in camp with her husband until the British surrendered their claim on the colonies. Other soldiers' wives spent part of the winter of 1777–78 with the Continental Army, and they had no better model than the general's wife, the future first lady of the country.

Part 2

First Ladies with a Cause

Veterans demanding early payment of small bonuses were among the first groups to march on Washington. [THE BEF NEWS]

7

Lou Hoover

The Bonus Army

As he removed his dinner jacket, Herbert Hoover turned to his wife and remarked: "You are mighty quiet tonight, my dear. Something must be troubling you. What is it?"

"We find ourselves in strong disagreement so seldom that I hardly know how to cope with it."

The president smiled and responded: "We've been through some tough times together, and we never let outside influences come between us. Can't afford to do that now!"

"I know," nodded his wife. "But this time things are different. You have already put your views into the record, and I do not want to do anything that could damage your campaign."

"The Democrats have already done a lot to see that I win again," Hoover observed. "Of all the candidates from which they could choose, they picked Franklin Roosevelt almost as though they wanted to help me. What on earth could you possibly do to put me behind him?"

"I've made up my mind to visit Anacostia Flats tomorrow," Lou Hoover confessed. "I will dress inconspicuously and not identify myself; I simply want to see for myself the conditions in which the veterans are living."

"Go, if you must," Hoover sighed. "You'll find a band of ruffians who have come here to try to extort money from the U.S. Treasury. I cannot agree to any of their demands; to do so would betray the American people."

Herbert Hoover was unwilling to negotiate with American veterans of World War I but cheerfully opened the baseball season at Griffith Stadium in Washington.

After breakfast on a hot day in mid-June 1932, the first lady summoned her driver and directed him to take her to "the veterans' camp across the river." Although the distance was short, it gave her time to reflect on some of the woes facing the nation.

With about nineteen thousand men and women on the District of Columbia's unemployment rolls, more hungry persons were not needed in the city. Clearly, Hoover and his cabinet members were right on that score.

Reared in comfort and married to a self-made millionaire, Lou Hoover could not imagine what it would be like to support a family on the average U.S. weekly wage of sixteen dollars. Yet millions of people would gladly have gone to work at that figure.

It was unemployment, Lou told herself, that lay at the bottom of the present problem that threatened to grow into a crisis. She did not then know that the three hundred veterans of World War I who had left Portland, Oregon, a month earlier carried with them an average of less than a dime each.

Initially regarded as a harmless bunch of cranks, the men who traveled mostly in freight cars but sometimes on foot had announced their goal was to force Washington to give them now a bonus promised in 1924 to be paid in 1945.

At East Saint Louis members of "the Bonus Army" were forced off the boxcars by railroad officials. Eager to be rid of them, Illinois officials requisitioned a fleet of trucks to haul them to the Indiana line. Publicity over the incident attracted other veterans who began converging on Washington from every direction. By mid-June many of them were encamped near the Capitol, with the announced intention of staying until they received their money.

After crossing the Anacostia River, Mrs. Hoover signaled for her driver to pull to the side of the road. As she descended from the vehicle she scanned a bewildering array of makeshift living quarters that sprawled across a small flat plain.

Big cardboard cartons predominated, but a few bedraggled tents were scattered about, and trails leading to the riverbank suggested that some had dug shallow caves along the embankment. One grizzled fellow wearing a tattered army uniform was reading a newspaper in front of a piano-box home identified by a crudely lettered sign as the "Music Hall." Soon she noticed that numerous wives and some children were there also.

Soldiers who made up the American Expeditionary Force in World War I were paid less than the men who stayed home and filled civilian jobs. Hence lawmakers had voted a "bonus" of $1.00 per day for military service stateside and $1.25 per day for overseas service. Men comprising the Bonus Army were determined to wait no longer; they needed their extra pay right now.

At dinner that evening Lou did not wait for Herbert to ask about her day. Instead she poured out a vivid description of the abject squalor she found at Anacostia Flats.

"Something must be done and quickly," she urged.

"My hands are tied," the president responded. "Perhaps you have forgotten that nearly one-fourth of the national budget is already devoted to veterans and their needs."

"You don't need to remind me," she retorted. "I'll never forget that you were responsible for establishing the Veterans Administration. A great deal is being done for the men who fought for America and for democracy," she continued. "But there are thousands who have come out of sheer desperation. Unless you do something, and soon, serious trouble will develop."

Hoover nodded understanding and reminded his wife that he had refused to take out injunctions that would have prohibited the Bonus Army from camping in the capital. "I am powerless to instruct members of the district commission," he said. "These elected officials have the final word, and most of them have already said they want the veterans—if they really are veterans—out of their city."

"A few may be impostors, but most of these men have had military experience," Lou responded. "One look at their camp—pitiful as it is—shows that it has been set up like a temporary army base. But if your hands are tied, it's useless for me to say more."

Through daily reports in the *Washington Sun,* the first lady kept up with events as more veterans arrived every day. Soon they were estimated to number twenty thousand in addition to the women and children.

Lou even managed to get several issues of the "newspaper" published in the camp. Called the *BEF News,* it took its name from the fact that many who demanded bonus payments called themselves "members of the Bonus Expeditionary Force."

To her husband she expressed concern when she learned that a bill designed to give partial relief to the penniless veterans had failed in the Senate after having been passed by the House. Some of her concern was alleviated when the president told her that his backing guaranteed passage of a new transportation measure for Congress to appropriate one hundred thousand dollars to send the Bonus Army home.

That money was never spent.

On July 28 Lou Hoover was concerned to see that military forces were gathering on the north side of Pennsylvania Avenue. She counted what she believed to be four troops of cavalry and two regiments of infantry. Then six tanks rumbled into the formation.

A clash between the district police and the veterans left one ragged former soldier dead and another seriously wounded. Cavalrymen with drawn sabers then entered the buildings occupied by the squatters. After evicting the former veterans from the buildings, the military contingent headed toward Anacostia Flats. Paul Y. Anderson of the United Press published an eyewitness account of what followed: "Men, women and children fled shrieking across the broken ground, falling into excavations as they tried to avoid the rearing hoofs and saber points. Meanwhile, infantry on the

With the U.S. Capitol as a helmet, Hoover was satirized as "an American Kaiser." [THE BEF NEWS]

south side who had adjusted their gas masks were hurling containers of gas into the packed mass of now-frightened squatters."

Soon egg crates, cardboard, and canvas in the "tent city" went up in flames. Veterans and their families were herded across the Maryland state line, then hastily shipped to a temporary camp in Pennsylvania. Many of them eventually returned to their homes, but others disappeared into hobo jungles and increasingly prevalent "shack cities" that were the only havens available to the unemployed.

Although she never spoke to reporters about the Bonus Army in later years, Lou Hoover occasionally shared some of her experiences with relatives and intimates. To them, she confessed that she was the only person from her husband's administration known to have paid even a brief visit to Anacostia Flats.

"I don't like to remember," she said. "To this day, I am ashamed that I was acquainted with or knew several of the officers who directed the assault upon the veterans' camp. Our U.S. Army chief of staff was on hand to see the job well done; to my knowledge,

Gen. Douglas MacArthur has never expressed regret at his role. I soon lost track of two other officers whom I considered splendid examples of our military forces. Maj. Dwight D. Eisenhower and Maj. George S. Patton were among those who in 1932 attacked and burned the camp occupied by unarmed veterans of World War I."

8

Elizabeth Monroe

The French Obligation

*P*artly because she spoke French fluently, the wife of the U.S minister to France spent much more time in shops and on the streets that did her husband. Nearly every day she learned of developments not reported through diplomatic channels until days or weeks later.

In February 1795 she spent hours trying to avoid her husband, who noted in a memo that she was "in the midst of one of her great huffs." Determined to end the silent quarrel, James Monroe spoke firmly, "You have said little or nothing to me in days; do tell me what makes you so unnaturally silent."

"I'm afraid that you will be displeased, but I have made up my mind to act."

"Act?" inquired the diplomat. "What madcap scheme do you have in mind this time?"

After a long pause his wife responded slowly but firmly, "I shall attempt to secure the release of Madame de Lafayette . . ."

"Why didn't you say so earlier? Perhaps it is a foolish scheme; we have been here less than six months and I do not yet know how these folk think. Yet I must confess that I admire your courage, and if I spoke the language well I would make the attempt myself."

Surprised and delighted, Elizabeth embraced James wordlessly. Before they reached Paris they had learned that the Marquis de Lafayette, French hero of the American Revolution, had fled the

Elizabeth Monroe was an intelligent, quiet, reticent person whom many people considered aloof. Deteriorating health limited her activities as first lady, which contrasted greatly with her predecessor, Dolley Madison.

country to avoid imprisonment but was being held captive in Austria. Once in the glittering city they discovered that the lives of the marquis' wife and children were threatened.

Unlike the colonial struggle in America, the French Revolution was largely a revolt of the dispossessed against persons of wealth and power. The revolution had given way to a reign of terror in which notable aristocrats were sent to the guillotine for crimes against the citizens of France.

"It is common knowledge that your predecessor warned the French that the execution of Madame de Lafayette would be regarded as an affront to the United States, yet he was unable to secure her release from prison," Elizabeth told her husband. "I am determined to do what I can; with your help, perhaps a miracle may be worked."

In the Plessis Prison in Paris, Madame de Lafayette and other inmates spent their days in terror; at any moment they could receive notice they were being sent to the guillotine.

Monroe, who liked the situation no better than did his wife, was hesitant to act. He feared that his effectiveness as the chief representative of the United States might be jeopardized if he meddled in the internal affairs of France. Nevertheless, once he realized

The Marquis de Lafayette was every bit an aristocrat as depicted in this painting at Versailles. [J. B. COURT]

that his wife had made up her mind to act, regardless of consequences, he gave her his wholehearted support.

Later the ambassador penned a lengthy memorandum in his day book, using his customary third-person style in referring to himself:

> There were then no private carriages in Paris [they having been outlawed] and the hacks were generally in the worst state. Mr. Monroe procured a carriage of his own as soon as he could, had it put in the best order, and his servants dressed in like manner. In this carriage Mrs. Monroe drove directly to the prison in which Madame Lafayette was confined. As soon as it entered the street, the public attention was drawn to it, and at the prison gate the crowd gathered around it. Inquiry was made, whose carriage is it? The answer given was, that of the American Minister. Who is in it? His wife. What brought her here? To see Madame Lafayette.

At the prison, keenly aware that she might be arrested and thrown into a cell, Elizabeth Monroe sought out the concierge and asked to see the distinguished prisoner. To her surprise, there was no difficulty and she was promptly led to the wife of the marquis who had done great service for the American colonists during the earlier revolution. What passed between the two women that day is a matter of conjecture, as no written record of their conversation exists.

Word of Elizabeth's daring exploit probably reached some members of the Committee on Public Safety within hours. A groundswell of admiration for *la belle américaine,* as she was called, could not be ignored. Soon Madame de Lafayette was released without condition.

As news swept through the city and then the countryside, many observers expressed surprise. Several female relatives of Madame de Lafayette had already been executed. Her husband was a member of the hated aristocracy. Why should the woman be set free simply because *la belle américaine* displayed interest in her?

That question, tossed about the streets of Paris and other French cities in 1795, was never answered. Perhaps the masses of ordinary French citizens were weary of the bloodletting. Perhaps her release was a sign that the leaders of the revolution were also anxious for a more normal atmosphere. Whatever the case, the actions of Elizabeth Monroe were without parallel. No other first lady has effected the release of a state prisoner.

In 1795 Elizabeth Monroe was too busy to think of herself as a heroine; the woman whom she had rescued needed help in getting her son out of the country. "It will be no small task," James Monroe warned. "If he manages to get a passport, he will never be permitted to return."

Elizabeth agreed, adding, "I think I may have a solution."

Soon George Washington de Lafayette was on the way to Le Havre with a passport in the name of George Motier, his father's surname. Placed aboard a small vessel by a friend of the Monroes, the son of Lafayette carried with him a letter from his mother to the man for whom he was named. To George Washington, Madame de Lafayette wrote, "Monsieur—I send you my son [whom] I now place under the protection of the United States, which he had long been accustomed to regard as his second country." She was eager for her son's education to be resumed, she continued. It was her fervent desire that Washington himself should guide George "with the sole object of fulfilling the duties of a citizen of the United States."

In Philadelphia, the president received advance notice that George was sailing westward. He quickly made arrangements for young Lafayette to be sent to New York to live with a one-time aide-de-camp of his father, La Colombe.

George Washington never explained why he chose for his namesake not to reside in Philadelphia, the nation's capital. Perhaps the answer lies in the observation of André Maurois: "Statesmanship has reasons of which the heart knows nothing."

There is no certainty that Elizabeth Monroe learned how the son of the woman she liberated was treated. Had she known that the president did not want him nearby, the future first lady might have staged another visit—this time to Philadelphia to confront the president.

9

Eliza Johnson

Time to Forget

*C*ouldn't sleep last night, Andy."

Startled, Andrew Johnson laid his pen aside and turned to his wife who had slipped quietly into his office. Usually she addressed him as "Pa." Any time she used his given name, she was likely to be upset about something.

"Have you had your breakfast?" he responded.

"Sure did, like always, but I didn't eat much; I wanted to get here early."

After a leisurely solitary breakfast, the first lady normally went to her husband's office where she spent thirty minutes or more helping him to check his schedule for the day. Although seldom seen by the power brokers of the capital, the diminutive gray-haired woman from the hills of Tennessee was known to be highly influential. One observer commented that she "seemed to exert a silent power over the president."

A Washington correspondent for the *Chicago Republican* stressed her infirmity rather than her persuasive power and described her as "a confirmed invalid." Pointing out that "her very existence is a myth to almost everyone," the newspaper told readers: "She was last seen at a party given [for] her grandchildren. She was seated in one of the Republican Court chairs, a dainty affair of satin and ebony. She did not rise when the children or older guests were presented to her; she simply said, 'My dears, I am an invalid,' and her sad, pale face and sunken eyes fully proved the expression."

Eliza Johnson was a fearful, reluctant first lady. She had nightmares of her husband being assassinated like his predecessor, Lincoln. Her reluctance was based in part on her belief that she was inferior to city-bred "society" ladies.

Invalid or not, there was no denying the power of Eliza Johnson's character and person. This was the same woman who in 1861 had refused to accept amnesty from the Confederate government in East Tennessee and had angrily refused the deportation of herself and her family to the North. As one of the majority of settlers in East Tennessee who had opposed secession, and as the wife of a man who as Union military governor in Tennessee was regarded by most Confederates as a traitor to his region and heritage, she defied Confederate authorities. Although the male members of her family had been threatened on several occasions and she herself had been the subject of numerous official communications, Eliza Johnson had stubbornly and steadfastly ignored Confederate military orders for more than four months. No other woman is known to have figured so prominently in documents later published as *War of the Rebellion—Official Records of the Union and Confederate Armies* (known simply as *OR*).

On a March morning in 1867, with Johnson's term of office due to expire in less than twelve months, everything in her demeanor suggested that the invalid was stronger than her appearance suggested.

"What's bothering you this time?" Johnson inquired.

Jefferson Davis, former president of the Confederacy.
[J. C. BUTTRE ENGRAVING]

"I've been doing a lot of thinking. You won't be the president much longer. Folks say General Grant is a hard-hearted man. He's a shoo-in for the White House, come November, so I've changed my mind about Jeff Davis."

"Just what do you mean by that, Mother?"

Acting as though he had no recollection of one of their White House clashes of will, Eliza gave him a capsule account of the 1865 period when he was making up his mind about amnesty for former Confederates. Adapting a plan earlier devised by Abraham Lincoln, his successor in office acted to facilitate reentrance into the Union of seceded states. At the same time, he extended amnesty to many leaders of the Lost Cause.

Johnson, as a former military governor of occupied Tennessee, had leaned toward including Jefferson Davis, the former Confederate president, in his proclamation. Partly because she had suffered torment at the hands of Confederates, his wife persuaded him not to take that step.

Captured in Georgia while attempting to flee from the country in 1865, Davis was branded a traitor. Clapped in irons, he was shipped to Fort Monroe in Virginia aboard the steamer *Clyde*. He requested a speedy trial and expected to get it, but he soon discovered that although he had been indicted at least three times, Federal authorities were not prepared to take him into court.

Fort Monroe, Virginia, where Davis was imprisoned.

Casemate Number Two at Fort Monroe had been fashioned into a special cell. There the former president of the Confederacy was forbidden to send or to receive mail. After many months, an ardent supporter of the Union cause became interested in the plight of Davis. Horace Greeley, publisher of the influential *New York Tribune,* launched an editorial crusade on behalf of the prisoner. Whether or not Eliza Johnson saw and was influenced by some of Greeley's editorials is not known.

During a lengthy conversation that sometimes approached the level of heated argument, the first lady urged her husband to take action "before it is too late." She knew that any move designed to result in the release of Davis would create a storm of controversy. That would be nearly nothing, she pointed out, in comparison with the impeachment attempt against her husband that had failed by a single vote.

Johnson responded to his wife's plea with enthusiasm, after having let her talk as long as she wished. Had it been left up to

Andrew Johnson of Tennessee was persuaded to launch the tradition of giving presidential pardons at Christmas.
[NATIONAL ARCHIVES]

him, he would have ended Davis's imprisonment months earlier. High-placed officials in his administration were adamantly opposed to such a move and made it clear that if he took it his life would be made miserable. Now that he had less than a year to serve, he felt he could live with whatever blame might be attached to his decisions.

As a result of a change of mind on the part of a fifty-five-year-old woman who suffered from tuberculosis and probably weighed less than a hundred pounds, a message reached Fort Monroe on April 28, 1868. According to it, President Andrew Johnson was willing to grant a pardon to Davis if he would make formal application for it.

Soon a writ of habeas corpus was issued, and after 720 days in prison, Davis departed his cell on May 10, 1867. Three days later, in Richmond, military authorities surrendered him to the custody of civil officials. They immediately asked that a judge presiding over the U.S. district court establish the amount of a bail bond which would have to be posted to deliver him from custody.

Judge John Underwood, keenly aware of emotional currents in the nation, set the bond at the then astronomical figure of one hundred thousand dollars. Some former Federal military officers who were present cheered when the sum was announced; they were positive that nowhere in the former Confederacy would it be possible to get a secured bond in that amount.

They were right, but they did not take the entire nation into account. Led by Greeley, a group of wealthy northerners promptly signed the bond.

Davis, scheduled for trial in the fall, soon took his wife to Canada. There he announced plans to write a lengthy book about the secession movement and his role in it. When he returned to Richmond, the judge who was presiding over the case announced that it would be postponed until March 1868. Additional postponements followed, leading a despairing Davis to wonder if he would ever have his legal leg irons and handcuffs removed.

He probably never knew that Eliza Johnson once more intervened on his behalf. Aware of Davis's plight as the Christmas season approached, she again addressed her husband as Andy. Now knowing that Lt. Gen. U. S. Grant would become president on March 4, 1869, Johnson issued a proclamation of universal amnesty. Under its terms, the foremost leaders of the Confederacy, Davis included, were eligible for full pardons.

Bonfires were lighted throughout the Cotton Belt, where Johnson's action helped to heal some of the wounds left by civil war. People who celebrated in Mississippi, South Carolina, Florida, and other states did not know that behind the scenes a woman from Greeneville, Tennessee, had pulled some strings to get the pardon.

As a result of the precedent set by the president who acted on his wife's advice, numerous other prisoners have been set free during the Christmas season. Warren G. Harding pardoned twenty-four on December 24, 1921. Twelve years later, Franklin D. Roosevelt proclaimed a Christmas amnesty for fifteen hundred men and women who had violated the Espionage Act during World War I. Harry S. Truman issued blanket pardons for large groups of offenders at Christmas in 1945, 1947, and 1952.

In 1868 few people were aware that subordinates of Jefferson Davis had banished Eliza Johnson and her family in May 1862 and made them homeless refugees. Tranquil enough to forgive her worst enemy in the face of what she considered to be impending death, Eliza Johnson clung to life for eight years after Davis became a free man as a result of the first presidential Christmas pardon.

10

Julia Tyler

The Texas Triumph

When President John Tyler married twenty-four-year-old Julia Gardiner, the couple became the subject of many jokes. John Quincy Adams described the October-April union as "the laughingstock of the capital." Journalists who knew that Tyler strongly favored the annexation of Texas quipped that the bridegroom soon to be fifty-four years of age had "succeeded nicely in at least one of his annexation schemes."

Although aware of the laughter, Julia ignored it and began poring over newspapers and books to learn more about her new husband's background and opinions. "I have turned my back upon New York and aim to become a thorough Virginian," she told one of her brothers.

Before her marriage on June 26, 1844, Julia realized that some old friends would turn their backs upon her if she pursued such a course. Many in New York were proud that theirs was a free state in which slavery was not permitted. Most informed Americans knew that Virginia included at least as many black slaves as free whites—perhaps more.

Somewhat to her surprise, the bride who was eager to adopt the views of her husband found that his interest in Texas was not necessarily linked with support of slavery. He was eager to enlarge the nation's commerce and saw Texas as the prime spot at which U.S. cotton could bolster its world monopoly. Years earlier he had gone

The death of Abel P. Upshur in the Princeton *disaster allowed Tyler to name John C. Calhoun (right) as secretary of state. Calhoun, like Tyler, was anxious to add Texas to the union.*

on record as supporting what would become a popular theme of the period, manifest destiny.

The expression first appeared in print in 1845 in the *Democratic Review,* when editor John L. O'Sullivan wrote, "Our manifest destiny [as Americans] is to overspread the continent allotted by Providence for the free development of our yearly multiplying millions."

A glance at a map showed that the United States was far from overspreading the continent. Between Kansas and the Rio Grande, the immense Republic of Texas covered an area of more than 376,000 square miles. On the southern portion of the west coast, Spanish California held every important port. In the Northwest, the question of the boundary of Oregon threatened to kindle a new war with Great Britain.

Strongly encouraged by his bride, the president who had been rebuffed repeatedly about Texas made up his mind to try once more to bring about annexation. He had a strong ally in John C. Calhoun, his newly confirmed secretary of state. Previously he had found little support in his cabinet on this issue because Texas statehood was viewed by northerners as encouraging the expansion of slavery.

In February 1844 Abel P. Upshur, Tyler's secretary of state who was against Texas annexation, had been killed in the same accident

Julia Tyler served as first lady for less than eight months. [ANELLI PAINTING]

that took the life of Julia's father and facilitated the introduction of the president and his future wife. Momentarily more interested in courtship than statesmanship, Tyler chose Calhoun to replace Upshur on the advice of several aides.

Since Calhoun was perhaps the nation's most persuasive proponent of the territorial expansion of slavery, his views quickly polarized the Texas question. Some senators who had previously supported annexation, now changed their position. To make matters worse for Tyler, he lost his bid for election, having succeeded to the presidency when William Henry Harrison had died only one month into his term of office.

"Never mind," Julia told her husband one evening when the president received an especially gloomy assessment of the situation. "You will still be president until James K. Polk takes the oath of office. If the Senate continues to balk, surely there must be some way to bring Texas into the Union without their consent before March 4."

Tyler's Fourth Annual Message to Congress, delivered in December 1844, included strong and persuasive language concerning "the Texas question." Julia helped to circulate copies of the document to relatives, supporters, and friends. "You still have more than two months," she reminded her husband as the year drew to a close.

John Tyler was elected to the presidency as a member of the Whig Party but once in office he repudiated the party platform and eliminated any chance for reelection.

By this time both the president and the first lady knew that the House of Representatives favored annexation. In the Senate—partly because of widespread antipathy toward John C. Calhoun—the climate was quite different. There it would take a miracle to win approval of the president's most cherished measure.

Tyler had come into office following an unprecedented but constitutional course of action on the death of the elected president. Were there similar options regarding Texas?

Julia Tyler was renowned at problem solving. Perhaps at her suggestion the president decided to bypass time-honored procedures involved in ratifying treaties. This process required a two-thirds vote in the Senate, and Tyler knew that the Texas treaty would never pass. Instead he told aides that if Congress could bring about a joint resolution in favor of the annexation of Texas, he would sign the measure into law.

The plan received overwhelming support. On February 27, 1845, the Senate finally put the all-important measure to a test that drew twenty-seven yes and twenty-five no votes.

"Had a single friend of Tyler and Texas changed his mind, all would have been lost," Julia reflected. Embracing her husband, she exulted: "That didn't happen! All is glorification!"

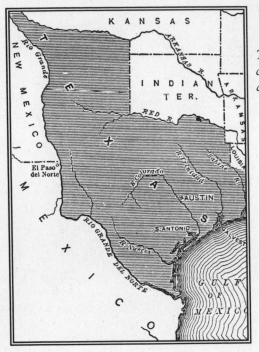

This map shows the area claimed by the United States as a result of the annexation.

Conventional processes having been circumvented, Tyler approved the Texas annexation measure a day before Polk's inauguration. Having used a special gold pen for the ceremonial signing, the Virginia-born chief executive presented it to his wife as a token of appreciation for her role in the long-drawn political fight.

Julia Tyler of Long Island, New York, bought a sturdy chain and had the pen fastened to it by a jeweler. Although her inherited wealth had brought her many diamond pendants, for the rest of her life she wore her Texas pen whenever she appeared at a formal dinner or reception.

11

Rosalynn Carter

Hard Hat, Soft Heart

*R*osalynn Carter, wife of the thirty-ninth president of the United States, was afraid that her uncertainty showed in her face. Surveying a gutted rundown building in a Manhattan slum, she decided that perhaps she could help remove trash.

Her husband, who was foreman of a crew of volunteer workers, had other ideas. Having arrived the previous day, he had already drawn up a work plan. "Go to the second story," he directed her. "The floor's about to cave in; we'll have to use plywood."

So the five-foot-seven-inch woman who had become his bride at age nineteen started toward what was left of a stairway. "Don't be in such a hurry!" Jimmy Carter called. "The first step is to clean the old floor. While that's being done, we can find out how many joists will have to be replaced."

According to a volunteer who has worked with the Carters on several of their construction jobs, "the former first lady did not bat an eye when she was handed a hard hat; she just put it on, straightened her Habitat for Humanity T-shirt, found a scraping tool, got down on her knees, and went to work."

Late the following afternoon, however, she temporarily balked when the floor foreman—her husband—handed her a hammer and gestured toward a sheet of plywood. "Take that to the far corner and nail it down," he directed.

Rosalynn later said that she felt temporary panic. Before they left Georgia, she had said that she would try to do just about

73

Rosalynn Carter moves plywood sheets while helping to renovate a gutted building on Manhattan's lower east side.

anything except use a hammer. Yet this was no time to remind Jimmy of that conversation; he was so happy to see the work going well that his eyes gleamed with delight.

That sheet of plywood was so big that she walked awkwardly when moving it, but the woman born and reared just outside the village of Plains, Georgia, lugged it to the designated spot. Seizing a hammer, she held a nail in place with her left hand, gripped the hammer tightly, took careful aim, and gave the nail a gentle tap.

Recalling later what was to her a traumatic moment, she laughed and said that it must have taken her at least a dozen strokes to drive that first nail. A photographer soon arrived, eager to get a shot of the only former mistress of the White House known to have helped build a house. After he left, she returned to work with zest and glowed when she soon learned to drive a nail with only a few strong strokes.

From early adolescence she had been accustomed to doing "women's work" only. In the southwest corner of Georgia where Rosalynn grew up, driving nails was a man's job.

Her father, who owned a farm about nine miles from the county seat of Americus, could not make a living from the land during the 1930s. Hence he repaired cars and also drove a school bus. His death in 1940, when his daughter was thirteen, was devastating.

Rosalynn had already learned to look after the family cow and to hoe the garden. She had been sweeping the porch for years and had been helping to wash and dry dishes since she was old enough to reach the sink.

Now she took over more of the household chores, since her mother spent much of her time as a seamstress when she was not working in a nearby grocery store. Keenly conscious of how hard life was for her widowed mother, Rosalynn was extra careful about her clothing. Neighbors marveled that "the Smith girl could wear a stark white dress all day long and not get it a bit dirty."

She practiced at home and became adept enough to get a part-time job at a beauty parlor, where she shampooed hair. Her mother eventually moved up to "a fairly good job" at the Plains post office; inevitably, this gave her daughter even more responsibility at home.

On special days some of the merchants in Plains flew their Confederate flags. In the northern tip of Sumter County, which includes Plains, Andersonville Historic Site now draws numerous visitors, and just to the north, in Macon County, a national cemetery holds the remains of thousands of Union soldiers who died of illness and starvation while in Andersonville during the Civil War.

When Rosalynn was a girl, nearly everyone around Plains was vaguely aware of the prison site, but neither white nor black young people took much interest in it. They and their parents were too absorbed with trying to keep food in their stomachs and clothing on their backs to pay much attention to what had taken place more than seventy years earlier.

Like virtually every other hamlet in the rural South, Rosalynn's hometown and the county seat were racially segregated. Blacks, most of whom were sharecroppers, had their own drinking fountain in the square at the center of Americus. They did not appear to consider it unusual that another fountain was labeled "Whites Only." Segregation was the way of life for members of both races.

Racially mixed neighborhoods and buildings were taken for granted in New York's Lower East Side, where Eleanor Rosalynn Smith Carter learned to use a hammer. She was pleased that an unemployed black man, who had lived in a cardboard box for months, was able to get one of the apartments built by Habitat for Humanity workers.

As mistress of the White House for the four years that began on January 20, 1977, she was said by some to be trying to be "a

Rosalynn Carter as mistress of the White House. [THE WHITE HOUSE]

second Eleanor Roosevelt." That was nonsense, she told reporters, although she confessed that she greatly admired her predecessor.

Soon after taking up residence in the White House, the new first lady attended a concert at New York's Carnegie Hall. That evening, she said she felt "a trifle like Eleanor Roosevelt," because she sat beside Marian Anderson. Years earlier, FDR's wife had resigned from the Daughters of the American Revolution when they refused to allow the black singer to perform in their Constitution Hall in Washington, D.C.

Rosalynn never said so, but she must have felt that her husband partly made up for that indignity. The peanut processor from Plains, Georgia, invited Anderson to sing in front of the Lincoln Memorial at the time of his inauguration.

During the following year, Jimmy Carter was the first sitting U.S. chief executive to visit new nations in Africa. Rosalynn and their daughter, Amy, accompanied the president during the week-long state visit. Journalists reported that in Badagry, Nigeria, the first lady "won the hearts of the women of the city, with whom she quickly formed a friendly and informal relationship." The Carters had completely outgrown the culture in which they had grown up.

Soon after they left the White House and returned to the region of their roots, this pair of devout Baptists began looking at what they termed "good causes." Both of them were eager to find ways in which they could use their time and energy to benefit the unfortunate, "regardless of race or creed or ethnic origin."

While her husband was chief executive, they had learned "a smidgen" about Habitat for Humanity, whose headquarters are in Americus. It was there, they discovered, because Sumter County was the location of a utopian experiment launched during the Great Depression.

Koinonia Farms, staffed by volunteers from many states and several foreign countries, produced peanuts and pecans and the candy and fruitcakes that utilized them. All profits were channeled to indigent people.

Koinonia lured Millard Fuller to the region from Alabama. A successful attorney, Fuller decided that making more money was not a worthy goal. He and his wife visited interracial Koinonia Farms, talked at length with the founder, Clarence Jordan, and decided to throw in with him. During their stay of several years, one of their many activities involved helping to build homes for people who could not otherwise afford them.

The Fullers then decided to see if this specialized form of social activism could be practiced abroad. With a lot of faith and enthusiasm and three thousand dollars from Koinonia, they went to Mbandaka, Zaire, in 1973. After having built more than 150 houses in that city and having seen their idea expand into outlying villages, they established Habitat for Humanity.

As Fuller saw it from the beginning, the program would have to depend upon the work of volunteers and the prospective homeowners. Those getting a decent place in which to live are not offered charity. Instead, they contribute their labor and agree to repay the actual cost of building materials over a period of twenty years. Now worldwide in scope but still centered in Americus, the program has been responsible for the erection of tens of thousands of affordable homes both in this country and elsewhere.

Rosalynn Carter and her husband were deeply impressed with the fervor Fuller showed when he said his goal was "to make quality housing available throughout the world!" As a result, they decided to channel much of their own energy and zeal into Habitat for Humanity.

They have literally traveled the world in pursuit of their dream. At Puna in the high Andes, they found the same exhilaration they experienced earlier when helping to build in the slums of Chicago. After both Rosalynn and her husband became numbered among Habitat's "old hands," the former president learned that the black woman who had been his childhood nurse was living in a tumble-down shack. When Nanny Rhodes moved into her new Habitat home, newspapers everywhere ran stories about the event.

During their courtship, the future president and his sweetheart exchanged many letters that ended with a cryptic set of symbols—ILYTG. That was the way each said to the other, "I love you the goodest."

Decades later, the former president wrote, "My wife has never been more beautiful than when [she wears a hard hat] and her face is covered with smut from scraping burned ceiling joists and is streaked with sweat from carrying sheets of plywood."

12

Betty Ford

Quiet Crusader

$\mathcal{B}$etty Ford and her husband became White House residents under unique circumstances. Gerald Ford was the only vice president of the United States to become president upon the resignation of a chief executive. Only eight months before Richard Nixon resigned to avoid impeachment, he had appointed Ford as vice president, replacing Spiro Agnew who had resigned while under criminal investigation. Thus Ford became the only person to serve as vice president and president who had not been elected to either office.

A few minutes after Nixon departed the White House for the last time, at 12:03 P.M. August 9, 1974, a small party assembled in the East Room. Chief Justice Warren Burger administered the oath of office to Ford. When the ceremony was over, the thirty-eighth president said, "Our long national nightmare is over!"

Perhaps national stress over the Nixon White House ended that night, but for Betty Ford a long personal nightmare was just beginning. A month after moving into her new home, she underwent surgery for breast cancer, a radical mastectomy.

In 1974 the general public heard and read little about this procedure, and most people preferred to pretend that it was not practiced. Typical women who faced such mutilation of their bodies were quiet about it. The first lady was not typical, however. No other wife of a president had been a fashion model or a dance instructor. She was openly in favor of liberalized abortion laws.

First Ladies were often somewhat aloof. Some of them had issued strict sets of rules concerning the way they wished to be treated by White House staff members. Others had avoided everyday situations, preferring to be seen only under controlled circumstances.

During her husband's twenty-four years in the House of Representatives, Betty and the congressman from Michigan lived in Alexandria, Virginia. Of herself during those days, she said that she "looked after children and the household, shopped, and made casual acquaintances just like any other American housewife of the period." This set of attitudes and practices was not modified when Gerald Ford became House minority leader in 1965.

Mrs. H. Don Winkler, later a teacher but then also "an ordinary housewife," was married to a vice president of George Washington University. Now living at Hilton Head, South Carolina, she has vivid memories of encounters with Betty Ford in supermarkets, drug stores, department stores, baseball games, and Boy Scout gatherings.

"She was as casual as though her husband did not play a prominent role in lawmaking," said Mrs. Winkler. "We were not together on social occasions, but I saw her and spoke to her often enough to know that she has no pretensions whatever."

This appraisal by an acquaintance was echoed by reporters as soon as they got a good look at the new first lady. *Newsweek* magazine informed its readers, "Betty Ford will set a different style" and characterized her tenure in the White House as "sure to be folksy."

As soon as she received the medical verdict concerning her cancer, Betty began talking openly about it. Complete candor on the part of the first lady led to newspaper headlines throughout the nation. She was labeled a "quiet crusader for frank and open discussion of what was once a topic for closet conversation only."

Soon the impact of her decision to treat her mastectomy "just like any other medical procedure" bore unexpected results. Happy Rockefeller, wife of Nelson Rockefeller, whom Ford had appointed as his vice president, developed breast cancer. Inspired by the example of the former fashion model, she went to surgery with few if any qualms and upon her recovery insisted that she owed her life to Betty Ford.

Two years later, near the end of Gerald Ford's tenure as chief executive, the first lady received a dreadful verdict from her loved ones. Deep inside she knew that she was losing a fight with alcohol

Betty Ford consented to a press conference during her first month in the White House and impressed everyone with her candor. [GERALD R. FORD LIBRARY]

and prescription drugs. Yet it came as a wrenching shock in the pre-Christmas season when her husband and children told her that they had decided they must intervene: She must seek professional help soon.

Initially unwilling to consider such a course of action, she responded that she could cope with her problem without assistance. Looking back, she later characterized this period as "a fog that was sometimes euphoric, sometimes depressed."

Family members knew how difficult it would be to overcome alcoholism coupled with drug addiction without help. Hence they took her to Long Beach, California, soon after she returned to Grand Rapids, Michigan, from the White House.

A big sign reading Alcohol Rehabilitation Center evoked inner denial. That was not what she needed, Betty told herself; she was in search of help for her "pill problem" caused by prescriptions to relieve the pain of a pinched nerve in her neck. It took her more than a week to admit to herself that she was in the right place and badly needed help. She later wrote that she "was finally shocked into admitting to my peer group that I was alcoholic."

A decade later she wrote an autobiography entitled *Betty: A Glad Awakening*. In it she explained, "Alcoholism is a chronic disease." It is "treatable, but not curable," and it is progressive. A person may abstain for years, she noted, but when he or she again turns to drink "it's as though you had been drinking all those years."

At Long Beach, Betty Ford began practicing the twelve steps of Alcoholics Anonymous. There she also learned from experience how much a support group can mean to a person struggling to become free of addiction. A group of women who were also recovering from alcoholism met with her for an hour once a week. Some of them regularly made the long trip from Laguna Beach to be with her.

Discharged after four weeks of treatment, she is the first mistress of the White House publicly to admit waging a fight to overcome addiction. In doing so, she repeatedly stresses that she is in the process of recover*ing* and avoids saying that she has recover*ed*.

Once she and the stalwart husband she calls Jerry were guests at a dinner party at which an ice was served after a fish course. As soon as she tasted it, she realized that it was "straight champagne, frozen, and then mushed up." Reflecting upon that experience, she cautions readers, "For a recovering person, it's very dangerous to take that first bite, sip, slug, of anything alcoholic. Abstinence is the only guarantee of sobriety."

In 1978 Betty Ford became vividly aware of how difficult it is to deal with alcoholism. Continually in the process of recovery, the former mistress of the White House made numerous contacts with professionals who worked in programs designed to break the stranglehold of addiction.

To her consternation, she learned that 90 percent of people who have alcohol and drug problems are consigned to psychiatric hospitals. Most or all of them should be in facilities offering specialized care, but there are not many available.

As a result, President Gerald R. Ford's wife and a few professionals began dreaming of establishing a new and highly specialized place of treatment. That's how the Betty Ford Center came to be an adjunct of the Eisenhower medical complex in Rancho Mirage, California.

The former first lady did much more than lend her name to the center; she spent many months raising start-up money. While in the White House, she had used her quiet influence on behalf of the women's movement: liberalized abortion laws, appointment of a

Betty Ford's post–White House life has revolved largely around the center that bears her name.

woman to the U.S. Supreme Court, the Equal Rights Amendment, and similar causes. Today she serves as chairman of the center that bears her name.

The purpose of the center was expressed in her introspective volume *The Times of My Life*. She described herself as "always a nice enough woman" who walked, talked, and was polite when attentive. Then she admitted, "For a while, I had been unaware of how much went on around me, and I had no particular will to live." Great numbers of people "exist like that" but don't have to, since they can change. The Betty Ford Center was created for those "who exist like that."

During the fourteen years since the center opened, Betty Ford's keen personal involvement has increased rather than diminished. She has seen the capacity for residential patients jump from one building to four, each accommodating twenty persons.

Recognized as an international leader in the treatment of alcoholism and other drug dependencies, the Betty Ford Center has from its beginning emphasized the needs of women. Nationwide, physicians prescribe twice as many legal psychoactive drugs to women as to men, and this practice helps to account for the number of women who become addicted. Children from families with alcohol and other drug dependencies are particularly vulnerable. Hence the Betty Ford Center offers a special program for them.

Betty Ford, perhaps a bit more outspoken than "the quiet crusader" of earlier years, did not vegetate when she stepped from the spotlight of White House life into comparative obscurity. Instead, she found a life-consuming goal that she pursues with zest and enthusiasm.

13

Taft to Madison

Other Crusaders

Tokyo's Mayor Yukio Ozaki was puzzled when he received an urgent request from the wife of the president of the United States. She said that the District of Columbia was in need of trees. Not just any trees, but single white-flower cherry trees, known to the Japanese as *yoshino*.

After several messages were exchanged, Ozaki and his wife sent some trees to Mrs. William Howard Taft. Personal rather than municipal or state gifts, they reached Washington in such good condition that nearly four thousand of them survived. After insects and weather took their toll, their number was reduced about 10 percent. With thirty-five hundred Japanese cherry trees to her credit, Helen Taft goes on record as the tree-plantingest of all first ladies.

Mrs. Lyndon Johnson saw the now-famous cherry trees as symbols only. They beautified the Capitol area when in bloom, but did nothing for the rest of the district or the nation. Convinced that mounting crime and juvenile delinquency stemmed in part from squalid surroundings, she campaigned for what she called "a more beautiful capital" before going national.

During her tenure as mistress of the White House, Lady Bird Johnson traveled thousands of miles for ceremonial tree plantings. More than any other first lady, she persuaded ordinary folk to do their best to make America truly beautiful. In the process, she stirred up animosity among corporations in the mammoth bill-board industry, which she contended created eyesores along the interstate highways.

Earlier, Ellen Wilson made a street-by-street tour of the city designed to be one of the most beautiful in the world. Appalled at the slums she found almost in the shadow of the Capitol, she began badgering members of Congress.

Some lawmakers who were opposed to federal action aimed at reducing poverty yielded to the pleas of the first lady and enacted a housing measure informally called "Mrs. Wilson's Bill." It became a tribute to a seriously ill woman who would spend less than a year in the White House; Ellen Wilson died in 1914. Under the terms of the legislation, funds were provided for the erection of decent housing and demolition of badly decayed homes in what were then the worst slums of the District of Columbia.

Less than twenty years later, Eleanor Roosevelt, the first lady with the longest of all tenures in the White House, looked farther afield. Nowhere else in America, she realized, were housing conditions so appalling as in some portions of Appalachia. As a result, she conceived and executed a plan for the building of Arthurdale, a brand-new community for impoverished families of the southeastern mountains.

Among all first ladies, two tower above the others in their devotion to a cause. Lucy Hayes was so opposed to the use of alcoholic beverages that historians credit her with having made the Women's Christian Temperance Union respectable and powerful.

Hillary Rodham Clinton did not do so well with the crusade she headed. Opposition by a powerful insurance industry and many leaders in the medical field was enough to erect significant hurdles against her program of universal health care. Many analysts concur in the judgment that Hillary stumbled by presenting a plan so complex that its opponents easily scuttled it. Although she failed in her task, she is the first presidential wife assigned the task of writing a major legislative proposal.

Louisa Adams never launched a campaign or crusade; in her day such activities were reserved for men. She did go on record, however, as an ardent feminist before that word had been coined. If

*At age eighteen the future
Louisa Adams seemed to be
the epitome of feminism.*
[MASSACHUSETTS HISTORICAL
SOCIETY]

no one else learned her views, she clearly made them known to the president. The inferior status of American women, she told her husband, John Quincy Adams, should give the world's greatest democracy "about as much satisfaction as the badge of slavery, generally." Louisa said she had clear ideas of what Almighty God intended a woman to be "before she was cowed before her Master, man."

Lucretia Randolph, who was a schoolteacher—one of the few careers open to women at that time—hesitated to take the step that eventually led her to the President's House. She told James Garfield that she was truly fond of him but was not sure she wanted to marry him or anyone else. "My heart is not yet schooled to an entire submission to that destiny which will make me the wife of the one who marries me," she warned when she postponed setting a date for a wedding.

Administrators at the Johns Hopkins Medical School in Baltimore were pleased when they discovered that Caroline Harrison, Benjamin Harrison's wife, had expressed interest in the institution. When approached about helping to raise money for it, her response

Barbara Bush is especially fond of her signature three-strand pearl necklace. [THE WHITE HOUSE]

was conditional. Yes, she would approach some persons of wealth, she said, once the trustees of the school agreed to admit women.

Soon after entering the White House, Eleanor Roosevelt wrote a book with the self-explanatory title, *It's Up to the Women.* Her insistent urging that household servants should receive better pay caused her to become the most hated of first ladies among middle- and upper-class women of the South.

Rosalynn Carter was among the most conspicuous backers of the Equal Rights Amendment to the Constitution. It would have made "equal pay for equal work" mandatory, but it failed ratification by the states. In spite of this fact, the influence of the first lady helped to reduce the wage and salary gap between men and women.

Betty Ford initially devoted much of her time and energy to raising funds for the study and treatment of cancer. When the issue over soldiers classified as missing in action in Vietnam moved to center stage in the attention of the public, she became an enthusiastic volunteer worker for No Greater Love, whose goal was to help families locate their missing loved ones.

Dolley Madison was the first first lady to witness her husband's inauguration. During the Jefferson administration she served as White House hostess and helped raise funds for the Lewis and Clark expedition.
[GILBERT STUART PAINTING, PENNSYLVANIA ACADEMY OF THE FINE ARTS]

By the time Nancy Reagan became mistress of the White House, drugs were a national scandal. She spent a great deal of time and energy working for the Just Say No campaign. Her involvement in the campaign included prime-time appearances on television and chairing a conference on drug abuse attended by first ladies from around the world.

Barbara Bush became a feminine counterpart of Don Quixote by launching a campaign to make every American literate. She did not reach her goal, but her pursuit of it was responsible for helping thousands of adults to learn to read and write. She persuaded publisher Harold W. McGraw Jr. to join the movement and launch the Business Council for Effective Literacy.

Dolley Madison listened with wide-eyed wonder when Capt. Meriwether Lewis shared his dream of leading an expedition into what was then the uncharted Northwest Territory. A venture such as that needed strong financial backing.

"I'll help!" Dolley volunteered in 1802 after serving as hostess for a dinner given by the widower president. Years earlier, Jefferson had considered the possibility of organizing an expedition such as

Lewis had described. Financial hurdles lay in Congress, not the President's House.

Because she was perhaps the most admired woman in Washington, it was easy for Dolley to gain a hearing among the lawmakers. Serving as an enthusiastic unpaid and unofficial lobbyist—the first female to function in this fashion—she played a large role in persuading Congress to fund what became the Lewis and Clark Expedition of 1803–6.

When the explorers returned, she rejoiced at knowing that her country included countless natural wonders first seen by members of the expedition. Remembering how hard she had worked on behalf of Lewis and his comrades, however, Dolley never again launched a one-woman crusade for a congressional appropriation of any sort.

Part 3

First Lady Firsts

Grover Cleveland's marriage to Frances Folsom was the first marriage to a president in the White House, but had been originally scheduled to take place at the home of Frances's grandfather.

14

Frances Cleveland

A Private Ceremony

No member of the press will be permitted," ordered the president. "Attendance at this private ceremony will be limited to members of my family, the Folsom family, and members of the cabinet."

As a result of this restriction, only thirty-one people—including the bride and groom—were present at the first wedding conducted in the White House.

Oscar Folsom of Buffalo, New York, was killed in an 1876 carriage accident. His friend and partner, attorney Stephen Grover Cleveland, voluntarily assumed responsibility for Folsom's affairs. His greatest concern focused upon twelve-year-old Frances, who was inconsolable at the loss of her father.

Without assuming legal guardianship, the big man she called Uncle Cleve made most of the decisions that affected the girl's future. She must go to a good school, he directed. After graduation it would be well for her to spend a few months in Europe with her mother, making the Grand Tour.

During the years when little Frances was separated from Uncle Cleve, the two corresponded regularly. She did better than average work at Wells College in Aurora, New York, and won her diploma on schedule. Many of her classmates confessed that they wished they had her good looks.

She was customarily called "tall and thin and possessor of creamy skin" without her height being specified. The eyes of the

Grover Cleveland took his ward, young enough to be his daughter, as his bride in the first White House wedding ceremony. [LIBRARY OF CONGRESS]

college graduate were praised as being "sapphire-blue," and abundant wavy chestnut hair was her pride and joy.

Small wonder that forty-eight-year-old Uncle Cleve developed something more than avuncular interest in the raving beauty whom he had seen grow up. In secret correspondence he proposed marriage, she accepted, and both agreed that only their closest relatives would know of their plans until marriage arrangements could be finalized.

Usually addressed by Cleveland as Frank, early in the fall of 1885 his ward left for nine months in Europe with her mother. Cleveland's farewell message was a telegram that hinted of things to come.

Elated at having discovered that the president of the United States had marriage on his mind, a telegraph operator leaked the news. When the telegram was reprinted, many people assumed that Cleveland had developed a romantic interest in the widow of his partner.

Questioned, he gruffly responded that it seemed to him that folk might realize he could be interested in a younger woman.

The precise implications of his comment were lost on the reporters, who gave only brief attention to the story. Since Mrs. Folsom and her daughter refused to speak to a member of the press, little news filtered back during their long absence from the United States.

By the time their steamer approached New York on the return voyage on May 27, 1886, however, it was known that Frank Folsom expected to become the nation's first lady in early June. What was not widely known was all the reading and questioning that Frank had done during her tour abroad.

Before Frances and her mother began their journey, the bride-to-be accumulated a stack of newspapers. It would help the time to pass to read about the election of 1884, she believed. Besides, that would enable her to talk intelligently with Cleveland about his career after she became his wife.

She was pleased to discover that Henry Ward Beecher had supported her future bridegroom for the nation's highest office. This represented a change of stance, the famous clergyman told reporters. Initially he had frowned upon "some dark episodes in Cleveland life," but later he found that Cleveland's record was cleaner than that of his opponent.

Frances remembered that her father's former law partner did not fight in the Civil War, but she did not regard it as important that he had hired a substitute, which was a standard practice. She was gratified to learn that Gen. Carl Schurz, who was in uniform for more than four years, was among Cleveland's staunch supporters.

When she came across a cartoon entitled "Another Voice for Cleveland," she was startled. An eye-catching sketch intimated that "Grover the Good" might not be as good as folk thought.

Emma Folsom, her mother, frowned when Frances brought the cartoon to her. After a long silence, she explained that it referred to matters she preferred to forget. Puzzled, Frances persisted. Eventually her mother broke down and told her the story behind the cartoon.

When Grover was just twenty-two years old, she said, a woman who said she was a widow came to Buffalo. She was "quite ordinary in appearance" and at first attracted little attention. Calling herself an experienced collar maker, she soon found a job. Then she advanced to the rank of clerk in a store and manager of a department. Maria Halpin had moved west, she told her employer, because "no jobs were to be had in Jersey City."

A newspaper cartoon revealed something of Grover Cleveland's past to his bride-to-be.

Soon some wives of business and professional men of Buffalo began to wonder whether or not the newcomer really was a widow. She never wore mourning garb and always appeared to be lively and vivacious. Soon it was common knowledge that well-known men regularly visited her in the evening.

One of these visitors, Mrs. Folsom reluctantly explained, was Frances's father and another was her Uncle Cleve. Three years after reaching Buffalo, "the widow Halpin" gave birth to a child. She had no idea which of her half-dozen regular visitors had fathered the baby. On one score she was positive, though: having been discharged by her employer she had to have financial help.

As gently as she knew how to say it, Emma Folsom explained that "Grover took responsibility." Since he was the only bachelor among the intimates of Maria Halpin, it seemed to him the right and proper thing to do. He had no idea whether or not the baby boy was his, but he claimed paternity.

Judge Roswell L. Burrows was not positively known to have paid regular visits to Maria, but he displayed keen interest in her dilemma. At his suggestion, Cleveland arranged for the infant to be placed in an orphanage where he told the person in charge that he would be responsible for the fees of five dollars a week.

That's where the business would have ended, Frances Folsom learned, had it not been that the nation was in turmoil during 1884. Gen. Benjamin F. Butler, a noted veteran of the Civil War, was hinting that he would accept the presidential nomination for the Anti-Monopoly Party. Both the Equal Rights and the Prohibition Parties planned to put candidates into the field.

Despite being regarded as splinter movements, Oscar Folsom's widow explained, these political groups could be damaging. Although she had shown little interest in politics while in college, Frances indicated she understood. "Is that why the Democrats turned to Uncle Cleve?" she inquired.

Her mother nodded, then explained that the Republicans had selected James G. Blaine of Maine as their candidate. Having a spotless reputation and a strong national following, he would be difficult to beat. One month after he was chosen as the Republican standard-bearer, the Democrats met in Chicago and nominated Cleveland on the second ballot.

It was to discredit the governor of New York who had started his career as a law clerk at sixteen dollars a month that Republicans dug up the Maria Halpin story. According to Emma Folsom, the cartoon drawn by Frank Beard "created an immense sensation when it appeared." Soon, however, Democrats learned that Blaine had been married only three months when his first child was born. Circulation of derisive jingles concerning Blaine greatly blunted criticism of Cleveland.

Frances did not need to be reminded that her native state decided the election of 1884. Had a few thousand New Yorkers who voted for her Uncle Cleve backed Blaine or a candidate of one of the smaller parties, she would not now be on the way to Europe in order to slip away from newspaper reporters.

Before their ship docked, Cleveland's fiancée reached a firm and lasting decision. She was sorry that she had learned about Maria Halpin but could assess Cleveland's conduct only in retrospect. After all, a full decade—half of Frances's entire life—had passed since Halpin had given birth to a child who might have been fathered by any man who had visited her. Frances Folsom decided that Maria Halpin was none of her business.

Col. Daniel S. Lamont, secretary of war, performed many of the functions now associated with the White House chief of staff. Hence Cleveland sent him to New York, where he met the incoming ocean liner with a tugboat. Transferred to the tiny vessel, Frank and her mother found a carriage waiting for them at the pier. It took them to a Fifth Avenue hotel, the Gilsey House, where they registered secretly.

Frank and her mother were passengers on the early train from New York on June 2. Arriving before the sun was up, they were met by a White House carriage and spirited to the mansion. So far, their plans for the most part remained secret.

Those people whose business took them to the White House that day could not avoid noticing a great deal of unusual activity. Hundreds of plants and flowers were being taken to the Blue Room. Reporters who sensed the possibility of getting the story of a lifetime besieged Cleveland's office with requests that went unanswered.

Yet someone discovered or guessed that a 7 P.M. wedding ceremony was in the making. As a result the *Washington Post* editors urged their readers to unfurl flags, light up their homes, ring bells, and if possible, arrange for cannon to be discharged at the magic moment.

Throughout the nation, feature writers posed questions that they could not answer. Did the bride-to-be know that she was marrying a former sheriff who had presided over the hangings of condemned men? Was it possible that young Miss Folsom did not know that during the Civil War her husband-to-be hired a substitute to avoid military service? Most significant of all, what if anything did Frank know about the illegitimate child for whom bachelor Cleveland assumed responsibility years earlier?

Precisely at 6:30 that evening John Philip Sousa directed members of the Marine Band, wearing dress uniforms bright with red and blue, in a performance of Gilbert and Sullivan tunes. Twenty-eight guests were seated when the Reverend Byron Sunderland stepped before them. His impassive face revealed no clue to the fact that he would not follow the customary service. Only Sunderland, Cleveland, and Folsom knew that the president had written a special section of the ceremony eliminating the bride's promise to obey her husband.

Grover Cleveland and Frances Folsom were married in a ceremony in the
White House. A nervous Cleveland forgot to kiss the bride after the ceremony.
[LIBRARY OF CONGRESS]

Oblivious to bells ringing and chimes sounding throughout the capital, the bride and groom descended the grand stairway precisely at seven o'clock—without attendants. As soon as they were pronounced husband and wife, Lamont signaled for guests to move through the Green Room into the East Room. During half an hour, the happy couple received congratulations in what newspapers described as their promenade. Doors were then opened and the wedding party moved into the State Dining Room for a formal candlelight dinner.

Five years more than twice the age of the bride, the president personally had made most of the arrangements for the ceremony. Since he was not a member of any church, it would have been awkward to have a church wedding. Having been away for nearly a

Frances Folsom Cleveland was a gracious and cordial first lady who held receptions three times a week in the White House. When Cleveland was defeated for reelection in 1888, she bid the White House staff a tearful goodbye and asked them to take care of the house because they would be back. Four years later they returned, the only presidential couple to serve two nonconsecutive terms.

year, Mrs. Folsom and Frank were not eager to use their home. Ceremonies were often performed in luxury hotels, but Cleveland knew he could not completely control such a setting. That's how a bachelor chief executive decided in 1886 that for the first time the White House would be used for a wedding.

Once the newlyweds were in their private railway car, headed for Deer Park resort in Maryland, all attempts at secrecy were abandoned. Reporters drafted imaginary accounts of what took place in the Blue Room, then packed spyglasses into their bags and raced to Deer Park hoping to catch an intimate and exclusive glimpse of the nation's most famous couple.

In the capital, editors scoffed at Cleveland's demand for privacy and declared that it "does not suit the American people who, since the advent of modern journalism, have no private matters." Despite the fact that journalists who followed them on their honeymoon found little to report, the president was furious. He never quite understood how his plans for a quiet little wedding ceremony were thwarted. To the *New York Evening Post* he sent an indignant letter. Members of the press, he said, used their enormous power and influence "to perpetuate and disseminate a colossal impertinence . . . not to a private citizen, but to the president of the United States, thereby making American journalism contemptible in the estimation of people of good breeding everywhere."

15

Mary Todd Lincoln

A Traitor in the White House

We face a crisis without a precedent," Sen. Benjamin F. Wade of Ohio told colleagues who had assembled at Willard's Hotel. "A great deal of evidence suggests that there is a traitor in the White House. I think you know to whom I refer . . ."

Rep. Moses Odell of New York nodded his head, then stood up to speak. "No need to mince words, Senator," he declared. "I have had an eye on Mrs. Lincoln since the middle of March. We cannot watch her too closely."

"Her Confederate ties are so strong that we may be forced to take official action," Wade acknowledged. "Simon Cameron managed to get me a request addressed to him by Lincoln; I have enough copies for all of you to take a look at it."

The lawmakers who were meeting in an unofficial session accepted the sheet offered to them and read:

> Executive Mansion
> April 16, 1861
>
> Hon. Sec. of War
> My dear Sir
> Some time ago I requested that Ben Hardin Helm, might be appointed a Pay-Master, which I still desire. Next to this, for the sake of my friend, Major Hunter, I especially wish Robert A. Kinzie to be appointed a Pay-Master. This is not a formality, but an earnest reality.
>
> Your Obt. Servt.
> A. LINCOLN

Sen. Benjamin F. Wade wanted the Joint Committee on the Conduct of the War to question the first lady. [BRADY STUDIO, NATIONAL ARCHIVES]

"Cameron stalled, of course," Wade continued. "He never offered an appointment in Federal fighting forces to Helm. Good thing he did not."

"That's not the way I heard it!" exploded Massachusetts Congressman Daniel Gooch. "If my sources are right, Lincoln personally told this fellow that he could become a Union paymaster.

"Seems he turned the job down, flat, then went out and recruited men for a Secesh cavalry company that he promised he'd head."

"Your information may be correct, sir," Wade acknowledged. "In this White House, a great many things are done without entering the records. This much I know, for certain—by the time we assembled for our special session, Hardin was numbered among the prominent Confederates of Kentucky."

Heads were shaking and tongues wagged as men soon to become members of the Joint Congressional Committee on the Conduct of the War expressed their indignation and rage. Close relatives of the president's wife, of whom Hardin was only one of several, were preparing to take arms against loyal volunteers who had responded to the president's call for seventy-five thousand men to suppress the insurrection in the South.

Commissioned a colonel on October 19, 1861, Ben Hardin Helm was promoted rapidly. By the time he led his men against

The Executive Mansion, as Lincoln invariably called it, during the Civil War. The statue in front is of Thomas Jefferson. [NATIONAL ARCHIVES]

Union forces at Chickamauga in September 1863, he was a brigadier general. His death during that fierce battle triggered another wave of accusations against his wife's half-sister, Mary Todd Lincoln, when she ordered that the Executive Mansion be draped in black in mourning for him.

The daughter of a banker-lawyer-merchant whose family had helped to found Lexington, Kentucky, Mrs. Lincoln had other close relatives from that divided state serving in the Confederacy; indeed a majority of the extended family of the Todds had voiced their allegiance to the South. Mary's brother George was a Confederate surgeon. The husband of another half-sister, N. H. R. Dawson, also served in the Southern army along with three half-brothers who were later killed in battle: Samuel at Shiloh, Tennessee; David at Vicksburg, Mississippi; and Alexander at Baton Rouge, Louisiana. Since six close relatives were in Confederate service, it was not strange that the president's wife came under suspicion.

After having attended Hardin's funeral in Atlanta, his widow, Emilie Todd Helm, received on October 15, 1863, a pass from

Mary Todd Lincoln was a southerner by birth, and her relatives' unabashed support for the Confederacy led many to question her loyalties. [GODEY'S LADIES' BOOK]

Lincoln allowing her to go through Union lines. Initially thought to be headed for Kentucky, she decided instead to visit her sister in the nation's capital.

At Fort Monroe in Virginia, Mrs. Hardin was detained because she refused to take an oath of loyalty to the Union. At the insistence of his wife, Lincoln ordered that she be released and sent to Washington. With her daughter Katherine she then made her way to the White House for an extended visit.

After going home to Lexington, Emilie returned to Washington for a second visit in 1864. Putting her views in writing, she informed the president that "your minié bullets have made us [Southerners] what we are."

It has been said that Lincoln was deeply troubled by accusations that the White House harbored a traitor. In 1905 a supposedly reputable document was found that included an account of the president's visit to the Committee on the Conduct of the War. He was described as giving a vigorous but not entirely convincing defense of his wife's loyalty to the Union.

Recent scholarship has shown the tale of a sorrowful president confronting lawmakers to be bogus. Yet reports about the climate of opinion in Washington during 1861–65 are detailed and genuine. For four years, many a government official and ordinary citizen believed that Mary Todd Lincoln was secretly aiding and abetting the Confederate cause from the White House.

Several other members of White House families backed the South in the war. All three of Letitia Tyler's sons who survived to adulthood served the Confederacy. Robert, an attorney, was registrar of the Confederate treasury. John Jr., also an attorney, was assistant secretary of war. Tazewell, a physician, served in the medical corps. One son-in-law and several of the Tyler grandsons also fought for the South. Additionally, Richard Taylor, son of the deceased president Zachary Taylor, became a Confederate general.

In spite of the fact that her Southern ties were far from unique, among first ladies only Mary Todd Lincoln has been labeled a traitor to the Union. She publicly grieved over battlefield deaths and comforted a widowed sister. If she did more than that to aid the Confederate cause, records of such doings vanished long ago.

16

Margaret Taylor

Army Wife

Margaret Taylor, the most shadowy of the first ladies, was never captured on film. No artist painted a portrait sufficiently lifelike to be classified as official. She wrote and received letters, but two sent to her by her daughter are all that survive. During her White House days she met a number of notables but made little impression upon them.

From her June 21, 1810, marriage at Louisville until her husband, Zachary Taylor, took the oath of office in March 1849, Margaret was an army wife. In the nineteenth century, that meant that she rarely had a comfortable dwelling. Two of her five daughters died in childhood, and their three sisters and one brother saw very little of their mother. Unwilling continually to expose them to the hardships and dangers of frontier military posts, she sent them east to be educated.

Growing up in frontier Kentucky, Zachary Taylor had little formal education and enlisted in the army in 1806. At age twenty-four he received a commission as first lieutenant in the U.S. Army and never wavered in his conviction that life in uniform was the most promising career open to him. He moved from one remote post to another for three decades.

His bride cheerfully went with him to a place she had never heard of, Fort Snelling in the Michigan Territory (now Minnesota). Just one year later, she and her husband were at Fort Crawford (Prairie du Chien), where, to her surprise, she found there was a permanent four-room home for its commandant. About a dozen officers were stationed there, along with two hundred enlisted men who brought along a dozen women and two dozen children. According to a contemporary account, Fort Crawford's enclosure also included seventeen slaves.

Because Zachary was an experienced Indian fighter, he served in the Black Hawk War as a colonel and briefly was in charge of the captured Indian leader who gave the conflict its name. Once the fighting stopped, Colonel Taylor returned to Fort Crawford where Margaret rejoined her husband, along with their second daughter, Sarah Knox.

One of Crawford's young officers, not long out of West Point, took an interest in Sarah, but Margaret and her husband were opposed to their marriage. They did not want their daughter to spend her life going from one dreary army post to another. Despite their objections, however, Sarah Knox became the bride of Lt. Jefferson Davis. Davis resigned his commission and took his wife to the family plantation in Mississippi. Three months later, she died from "river fever" and Davis became a recluse.

Taylor, meanwhile, was ordered to Florida to quell a Seminole uprising. On Christmas Day 1837 he defeated an Indian force led by the renowned chief Osceola. The victory brought him a brevet (honorary) promotion to the rank of brigadier general, but living conditions for his wife did not improve. Life with Taylor sometimes meant living in a cabin in winter and in a tent during summers.

After a two-and-a-half-year campaign against the Seminoles in Florida, Taylor was reassigned to Baton Rouge, Louisiana. There Margaret chose for their quarters a picturesque cottage by the river and remodeled it into a comfortable home with a garden and a small dairy. Pleased with the results, the Taylors purchased it as a permanent home with a view toward retirement. The army, however, was not considering retirement for Zachary Taylor and promoted him to command of the Second Department of the Western Division of the U.S. Army, with headquarters in Fort Smith, Arkansas.

When war came with Mexico, "Old Rough and Ready," as Taylor was known to his men, commanded a ten-month campaign that won a series of victories, which included Resaca de la Palma and Monterrey. At a critical moment, half of his army was sent to bolster the forces of Winfield Scott in southern Mexico. The reduction, however, did not prevent Taylor's last and greatest victory of the war at Buena Vista on February 23, 1847. His force of

Mexican War hero Zachary Taylor was a natural candidate for the presidency. [LIBRARY OF CONGRESS]

forty-seven hundred men met a Mexican force of twenty thousand under Santa Anna and defeated it soundly. General Taylor was now a national hero.

Before the fighting ended in Mexico, Taylor was being approached by the Whig Party to accept its nomination to the White House. Although he took no interest in a political career now that his military career was concluding, at the 1848 convention in Philadelphia, he was nominated over Henry Clay, Daniel Webster, and his colleague in Mexico, Winfield Scott.

Margaret had been looking forward to retirement at the cottage in Baton Rouge, and she resented the fact that her husband had been taken from her again. Missing the companionship she had hoped for in retirement, she made no secret of her disappointment and accepted the role of a candidate's wife by having as little to do with it as possible. Taylor won the presidency primarily because the Democratic Party was splintered by Martin Van Buren's candidacy for the Free Soil Party.

During the campaign the opposition portrayed Margaret as a coarse farm woman with a pipe-smoking habit. After the inauguration Washington society was affronted that the new first lady was not interested in playing a social role and perpetuated the myth of the coarse farm woman. To the contrary, despite her husband's postings along the country's frontiers, both of the Taylors came from prominent families: Zachary's from Virginia, and Margaret's from Maryland. She was the product of New York finishing schools and also had a strong aversion to tobacco.

Margaret did not preside over White House dinners and levees, took little part in the Washington social scene, and spent most of her time knitting in a favorite upstairs room in the White House, which she had had decorated to match her room in Baton Rouge. Her youngest daughter, Mary Elizabeth Bliss, and the second wife of her former son-in-law Jefferson Davis, Varina Howell Davis, assumed any official duties that fell to the president's wife. Her lack of pretension was memorable to the second Mrs. Davis, who recalled that her most pleasant visits to the White House were spent in "Mrs. Taylor's bright and pretty room where [she], full of interest in the passing show in which she had not the strength to take part, talked most agreeably and kindly to the many friends who were admitted to her presence."

After the July 4 celebration in 1850, which included the laying of the cornerstone of the Washington Monument, Zachary Taylor became ill and died on July 9. Margaret resisted the proposal for an elaborate funeral for the Mexican War hero and also refused to have the president embalmed, hurrying the body to Louisville for a private ceremony.

Her actions seemed bizarre at the time, and rumors have persisted. As a result, Margaret Taylor became the first wife of a president to be accused of having poisoned her husband. The myth was dispelled when Taylor's body was exhumed and submitted to forensic scrutiny more than 140 years after Old Rough and Ready drank his last lemonade well laced with whiskey, but minus arsenic.

Margaret moved from the White House, not to Baton Rouge, but to her daughter's home in East Pascagoula, Mississippi. There her health declined, and two years after her husband's death, she died of a fever and was buried next to Zachary in Louisville. Her death prompted little notice to the public; her obituary in the *New York Times* did not even use her name, referring to her as "Mrs. General Taylor."

An army wife pure and simple, Margaret Taylor is the least known first lady. Deliberately inconspicuous, she can be dimly glimpsed only in the reflection from the polished scabbard that her husband wore at his side for most of his life. They were the first presidential couple to die before the president's term had been completed.

17

Abigail Fillmore

Book Lover

*N*ineteen-year-old Abigail Powers was not sure she liked the looks of her new pupil. Having had three years' experience in the classroom, the red-haired schoolmistress feared that a male student who looked at least as old as she might be a troublemaker. Besides, a new pupil would bring enrollment up to nearly twenty—making hers a large school.

Called to the front of the class from the back-row seat he had chosen, the newcomer gave his name as Millard Fillmore. Yes, he had some schooling earlier—from Webster's blue-back spelling book and the Bible. No, he did not expect to stay many months; he was there because the clothmaker to whom he was apprenticed was going on a journey. Sure, he thought he could learn a lot in maybe three or four months—and he knew how to keep his mouth shut when he was not called upon to answer a question.

Abigail reluctantly accepted Millard late in the winter of 1818 and quickly found that he posed no problems in the schoolroom. Matters of the heart were different; soon the pupil who was two years younger than his teacher was giving clear signals that he liked her, and not just as a teacher. She pretended indifference but did not discourage his overtures.

In the village of New Hope, New York, the brand-new academy conducted by Abigail was a local success story. She had moved there as a two-year-old with her mother after her father, Lemuel Powers, a backwoods Baptist preacher, had died. Among the few personal belongings they brought with them was his legacy of a small number of battered books.

By the time Abigail turned sixteen she was five feet four inches tall, well above the average height of mature women of the period. An acquaintance described her as being "commanding in person." That helped a lot when the girl who had received her education from her mother and from reading her father's books decided to open a school. No examination or license was required; she simply had to find suitable space and recruit enough pupils to make the venture worthwhile.

When she accepted Millard as a student, Abigail was unaware that she was conducting one of the better one-room schools of the period. Far to the southwest, nine-year-old Abraham Lincoln was spending a few weeks in what he later called a "blab school." Although he never explained the term, presumably he meant that the students blabbed, or spoke out, impulsively.

Millard carefully refrained from blabbing in the schoolroom. When he had a chance to speak with his teacher in private, however, he talked readily. While he was dirt poor, he was eager to learn because he was determined to practice law. Thus he applied himself without reservation to his lessons.

Abigail and Millard parted company after a few months when he had to return to work, but they wrote to one another regularly. Soon he shared with her the good news that his father, who was legally entitled to Millard's earnings as an apprentice, had chosen not to collect them from his son. Best of all, arrangements had been made for him to study law for two months at the office of a county judge.

When Millard demonstrated unusual ability, Judge Walter Wood of Montville encouraged him to set himself up as a teacher so as to increase his earnings. When he had thirty dollars in hand, he purchased his indenture and became Wood's full-time clerk.

Eight years after their first meeting, Millard Fillmore and Abigail Powers became husband and wife. By that time he was practicing law in East Aurora and aspired to a seat in the state assembly. In 1833 he was elected to the House of Representatives. Proving to be an astute politician, he soon began to advance through the ranks of the Whig Party, which he helped to establish in New York State, and was elected to three more terms in the House. In 1844 he was considered for the party's vice-presidential slot but became instead a candidate for the governorship of New York, which he narrowly

Abigail Powers and Millard Fillmore were engaged for five years while he completed his studies and became a lawyer. They were married in her brother's home when she was twenty-eight and he was twenty-six. [HENRY B. HALL ENGRAVING]

lost. Four years later he was nominated as Zachary Taylor's running mate, and the Whigs gained the White House.

Despite his political fortunes, whenever Millard was away from home for a few days, he always returned with a gift for his wife, not jewelry or clothing, but what Abigail wanted most—a book. When they moved into the nation's Executive Mansion following Taylor's death, Abigail was shocked to find that the house held no books—not even a Bible.

Since their son later ordered the burning of the papers and letters of Abigail Fillmore, documentary evidence concerning her accomplishments are scarce. As wife of the nation's thirteenth president, she showed an "independence of spirit" that some newspaper editors condemned.

The papers reported that she balked at the traditional restriction that the first lady never ventured outside the residence unless escorted by her husband. Jenny Lind, "the Swedish Nightingale," came to the capital for a concert and President Fillmore could not or would not attend. His courageous wife attended the concert enthralled.

In 1851 the Hungarian patriot Lajos Kossuth visited Washington soon after his release from a Turkish prison. His admirers arranged a civic banquet for him and announced that it would be

Henry Clay's measure to require free states to return fugitive slaves was vehemently opposed by Abigail.

attended by the president and his lady. Again Fillmore found it inconvenient to attend, but Abigail was there with her daughter in the seat reserved for the president.

Abigail's most unusual achievement attracted little or no attention at the time, however. Disappointed at finding the Executive Mansion bare of books, she prodded and persuaded her husband and his supporters to pass a special congressional appropriations bill earmarked for a White House library. With $250 made available to her, she transformed a second-story room into the first library.

Tastefully decorated and provided with a piano, it became what many guests considered to be the most delightful room in the mansion. Daniel Webster recorded his satisfaction at having spent an enjoyable evening in it.

Many late evenings in the presidential bedroom were presumably less pleasant. Henry Clay introduced into Congress the Fugitive Slave bill requiring free states to return runaway slaves. In appeasement to the South, Fillmore supported the measure. Abigail is believed to have warned him repeatedly that such a position would bring his political career to an end.

She was right. In 1852 the Whigs chose Winfield Scott over Fillmore as their candidate for the White House. Scott, however, lost the election to Democrat Franklin Pierce of New Hampshire.

Inauguration day, March 4, 1853, was miserably wet and cold, but Abigail considered it her duty to attend the ceremony. With William Makepeace Thackeray and Washington Irving as companions, she stood without shelter throughout the lengthy proceedings. Already having vacated the Executive Mansion, as soon as her official duties ended, she went to her room in Willard's Hotel and collapsed. Abigail Fillmore fought bronchial pneumonia for a month, then died in her hotel room.

18

Eleanor Roosevelt

A Royal Feast

Sara Delano Roosevelt was the bane of Eleanor's existence. Wealthy and despotic, FDR's mother held the purse strings and did not hesitate to wield her power.

Franklin began dating his fifth cousin, daughter of Elliott Roosevelt and Theodore's niece, about the time she made her debut. Sara was not enthusiastic at the prospect of having Eleanor as a daughter-in-law, yet when Franklin and Eleanor married in 1905, she made room for them in her Hyde Park, New York, mansion overlooking the Hudson River. During the summer season, her son and his wife lived next door to her at Campobello, an island between Maine and New Brunswick. When Sara learned that they expected to move to New York City, she immediately gave them a home there—and advice on any and all matters.

Thirty-four years later, with Franklin and Eleanor in the White House, the woman the president addressed as "Dearest Mama" was still trying to tell Eleanor what to do and how to do it.

One of her memorable letters was penned as soon as the Roosevelt matriarch learned that Great Britain's King George VI and Queen Elizabeth would visit Washington during the spring of 1939. President Roosevelt had invited them to make this side trip following their tour of Canada. "You must follow protocol to the letter," his mother instructed Eleanor. "It will be a disgrace to the nation if you fail to treat them as though they were in Buckingham Palace."

In an official White House photograph, Eleanor Roosevelt appears almost regal.
[THE WHITE HOUSE]

Royal visitors had been arriving at the mansion on the Potomac River for more than sixty years. One of the first reigning monarchs to visit was King Kalakaua of the kingdom of Hawaii. He was formally received by Ulysses Grant and his wife, Julia, on December 15, 1874, thirteen years before he gave the United States exclusive rights to use Pearl Harbor as a naval base.

Although the capital went all out for Kalakaua and for later heads of state, the expected arrival of the British royalty was in a category by itself. It was the first time a reigning English monarch had visited the former American colonies. "It is marvelous, so very marvelous," said a society matron of the capital. "People on both sides of the Atlantic will talk of this visit for decades to come!"

As is customary when British royalty travels, Buckingham Palace transmitted through diplomatic channels the specific requirements of the royal pair. These included an inkstand with a pair of inkwells holding blue black and red ink and, for the royal beds, eiderdown quilts and hot water bottles—the latter two being misguided requests for hot, humid Washington, D.C., in June. The first lady was confident that she would be prepared to receive her guests well before May.

On June 8, 1939, a twelve-car special train elaborately trimmed in gold and silver stopped at the Washington station. Wearing the uniform of the admiral of the fleet, the British monarch acknowledged the cheering crowds. Then he and his queen stepped into an open limousine already occupied by the president and his first lady.

After a twenty-one-gun salute was fired, their ceremonial journey to the White House took the form of a military parade. Bombers flew low over the capital whose streets were lined with half a million cheering Americans.

Events packed into the two-day royal visit were formal and subject to strict protocol. At the end of it, however, Eleanor spontaneously invited the king and queen to spend a few hours at Hyde Park before returning home. They graciously agreed to go there after spending a day at the New York World's Fair.

No one really knows why Eleanor Roosevelt decided to flaunt tradition at Hyde Park. She may have wished simply to assert her independence. Perhaps she was determined, for once, to do exactly the opposite of what "Dear Mama" had told her to do. Again, her announced intention of making it a "genuine American evening" may have been dominant in her planning.

At Hyde Park near the family home, in 1924 Franklin Roosevelt had provided the land for what he whimsically dubbed "a shack on a stream in the back woods" for "my missus and some of her female political friends." Far from being a shack, the stone cottage served as a hideaway for Franklin and Eleanor, but it was much more than that. Sitting beside the stream called Val-Kill, the center bearing that name became a focus for activities in which Eleanor was passionately interested. Her private Todhunter School was there, along with a furniture factory and the editorial offices of the *Women's Democratic News*.

It was at Val-Kill that Eleanor planned to entertain the royals. "You are likely to be surprised," she warned King George. "Instead of giving you another formal state dinner, I want you to see how ordinary Americans enjoy a leisurely evening."

Instead of engaging a famous entertainer for the evening, Eleanor asked a woman named Princess Te-Ata to sing some Native American songs. She invited neighbors and other local residents to join them for what she called simply "a picnic." The hostess acted as though she had never heard of protocol. Tables were arranged with care, but informally.

Eleanor Roosevelt, a world-renowned columnist, lecturer, and crusader, was a self-admitted bad cook. She claimed only to know how to cook hot dogs and scrambled eggs, which were served every Sunday evening. Even so, Eleanor only cooked the eggs; the staff prepared the mixture.

Although he had been warned that he would not be at a formal dinner, George VI was puzzled by the entrée. He inquired of his hostess, "What is the name of this delicacy?"

"It's a hot dog—the only food I know how to cook," Eleanor explained. "When I fix hot dogs Franklin and I eat them without special pieces of bread called 'buns,' which are made to hold them."

Eleanor's picnic was planned around a selection of typical American foods. Baked ham, smoked turkey, and baked beans came from a delicatessen, and strawberries were delivered from a Duchess County farm.

When bidding Franklin and Eleanor goodbye, in a rare moment of spontaneity, George VI invited his hostess to pay a visit to England. She accepted, but German forces invaded Poland three months later, and social plans were superseded by wartime needs.

"You have given us a delightful time," the monarch told Eleanor. "Until now, I had never tasted smoked turkey—which I find quite palatable. I must also confess I shall never, never forget my first hot dog. It is more firmly fixed in my memory than the marvels of the World's Fair."

When the last member of the royal entourage left, Eleanor Roosevelt went to her bedroom and opened her diary. Using a then-novel American-made ballpoint pen, she confided: "Well, one day is over and fairly well. The Queen reminds me of Queen Victoria. He is very nice, and doesn't stutter badly in quiet conversation."

19

Grace Coolidge

An Outdoor Christmas Tree

$\mathcal{M}$ost earlier renovations of the White House were modest by comparison with the work planned by Grace Anna Goodhue Coolidge. Although her husband was known as "Silent Cal," no intimate friend ever called her reticent.

She began talking about making changes in the presidential mansion soon after she moved in. As Warren G. Harding's vice president, Calvin Coolidge succeeded to the presidency at Harding's sudden death on August 2, 1923.

When Coolidge was elected to a full term in 1924, the first family felt completely at home in the White House. Earlier, Grace Coolidge had met frequently with wealthy and influential friends, among them Mrs. Harold I. Pratt of New York, whose fortune derived from Standard Oil Company. Mrs. Pratt derided what she called the "niggardly" congressional allotment for redecorating the mansion for the new occupants.

Possibly at the suggestion of Mrs. Pratt, Grace decided not to rely upon Congress, despite the fact that for her the redecorating appropriation had been raised from twenty thousand dollars to fifty thousand dollars. To get additional money, she turned to private donors and received from Congress permission to accept gifts of both cash and furniture.

Work began in April 1925 and continued throughout the summer. By fall the dwelling had taken on a new look that many found delightful. Decorations and furniture of European origin

Animal-lover Grace Coolidge persuaded her husband to light the first outdoor Christmas tree of the White House by promising that he would not have to speak.

were largely gone; for the first time in the twentieth century the mansion had much of the charm associated with colonial America.

Plans were made for an elaborate Thanksgiving dinner featuring only dishes used during the days of George Washington and John Adams and prepared from recipes known to have come from the period.

During the Thanksgiving dinner, the conversation turned toward the forthcoming Christmas holiday season. Someone recalled a project of interest to two of Coolidge's cabinet members: Secretary of the Interior Hubert Work of Colorado and former Secretary of Agriculture Henry C. Wallace of Iowa. Work and Wallace were promoting the fledgling Christmas tree farm industry and suggested that this new agricultural venture would get a boost if the White House became a showplace for decorated trees grown for market.

"There have been Christmas trees in the mansion many times," Grace remarked. "I believe Edith Roosevelt let Kermit put one in his room. She was an indulgent mother, and her five children knew how to get what they wanted."

Pausing for a moment, the first lady glanced out the window at the illuminated lawn. "I think we should launch a new tradition," she announced. "Let's erect a tall Christmas tree outside the mansion where the public can see it."

Coolidge was hesitant. He recalled that when he was a boy in Vermont, folk would have laughed at the idea of having a commercially produced Christmas tree. "We just went into the woods, picked out one we liked, then cut it and brought it home," he said.

Smiles on the faces of the men and women seated around the banquet table betrayed their reactions. Some of them had spent their entire lives in cities and did not know how to cut down "a proper Christmas tree."

Aware of their thoughts, Grace spoke up. "In order to please the president," she suggested, "we ought to secure a fine tree from a Vermont forest."

As heads nodded approval, she continued, "Ike Hoover [predecessor of today's chief of staff] can supervise its placement at a prominent spot. When brightly colored lights have been strung, we ought to have a ceremony in which the lights will be turned on."

That Thanksgiving night, the concept of an outdoor Christmas tree at the White House won approval. Traditional indoor trees were not omitted, however. A large one was erected in the Blue Room and a much smaller one went into the upstairs bedroom shared by the Coolidge boys.

Newspaper reporters began to write about plans for the National Christmas Tree, a label that caught the imagination of readers and became its permanent name. The numerous articles also sparked widespread interest in the ceremonial lighting of the tree.

At the last minute, the president seemed reluctant to play a role in the festivities. Grace dismissed his objections, reminding him that he was the first chief executive to give a radio address to the American people. "One more innovation will simply add to your reputation as a man not wedded to the past," she urged.

Silent Cal threw the switch that illuminated the first National Christmas Tree. Except during World War II, when blackouts were enforced in Washington, national Christmas trees have been central to the American observance of the Yuletide every year.

Since the advent of television, the lighting of the National Christmas Tree has been seen by millions of Americans. One element of the tradition has changed: in recent years, Fraser firs from North Carolina have been favored over the native trees of Coolidge's Vermont.

20

Jacqueline Kennedy

Superb Showmanship

*C*harles Collingwood, commentator for the television special, "A Tour of the White House with Mrs. John F. Kennedy," called the production "remarkable." His appraisal was one of the big understatements of 1962. For sixty minutes, three out of four American viewers—at least fifty-six million people—were transfixed before their televisions. Many noted that the "little girl voice" of the tour guide, who worked without notes, reminded them of the film star Marilyn Monroe. Some wrote letters offering to donate furniture, paintings, and memorabilia to the White House.

Thirty-four years later the Jacqueline Kennedy mystique demonstrated its potency. At Sotheby's in New York City, buyers engaged in what some called a four-day frenzy. The personal effects of the former first lady were on sale by her heirs to pay a part of the inheritance tax on her estate. The renowned auction house had estimated that the sale would generate four million dollars, but the final tally exceeded that amount by almost thirty million dollars.

A three-strand faux pearl necklace similar to the one worn by the mistress of the White House during the televised tour in 1962 was appraised at $500 to $700. When the auctioneer's hammer fell, the item had been sold for $211,500.

The assassination, mourning, and funeral of the thirty-fifth president accounts for only a part of the worldwide fascination with the first family of Camelot. Totally nonpolitical as a young adult,

Jacqueline Kennedy was one of the chief architects and queen of America's "Camelot" and looked every bit the part.

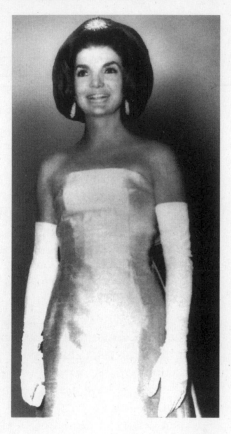

Jackie cast her first vote when her husband ran for the White House in 1960. Her interest in fashion, culture, and the arts was deep and genuine, hence the youngest first lady since the 1890s was one of the main architects of the Camelot era. Her husband was gracious in his welcome to Pablo Casals at the White House, yet it was Jackie who had invited him. Her trademark pillbox hats, bouffant hairstyles, and stack-heeled pumps were chosen by her, not by a fashion consultant.

At the end of the television tour of the White House, the husband of the tour guide made a brief appearance. There, for the first time publicly, he addressed his wife as "Jackie," a nickname she reputedly said she wished had never been devised. Little was said about the president's appearance, however. The focus of attention was more on the first lady. Her performance was graded as remarkable by director Frank Schaffner as she escorted the camera from room to room, seldom pausing in an easy flowing dialogue and making no mistakes of consequence.

One reporter for the *New York Times* was impressed by the intelligence and cultural insights of the first lady. Few had noticed her during the campaign addressing Louisianian Cajun crowds in French and Hispanics in the barrios of Southern California in Spanish.

The most striking impression made on the fifty-six million viewers was the manner in which the first lady offered spontaneous comments that revealed a wide-ranging knowledge of the furniture, paintings, and memorabilia throughout the White House. She also noted the donors of recently acquired pieces. Her casual manner belied the hours of preparatory work behind these comments interspersed with observations on all the presidents and families who had lived in the White House.

Gesturing toward a series of photographs of Lincoln, she pointed out how the sixteenth president had aged during the four years of the Civil War. She noted that Theodore Roosevelt had brought his fascination for the outdoors to the mansion by having numerous stuffed heads mounted in the State Dining Room, and then she added that Woodrow Wilson had so despised those trophies that he always arranged to be seated where he could not see them.

The first lady's knowledge of the White House, its inhabitants, and its furnishings was not casually acquired. A few days after her husband's inauguration, she met with artist William Walton and representatives of the National Gallery of Art. It was time to refurbish the White House, she told them, noting that the residence had become so sterile in appearance that some were comparing it to the Pentagon. She may have been motivated in her task following a 1961 trip to Bogotá, Colombia, where she was very much impressed with the old presidential palace.

Most or all of the furnishings and art in the White House should reveal something of the national past, she urged. Letitia Baldridge, the first lady's social secretary, recalled that Jackie "was determined to make the White House a showcase of American history and art."

The first lady knew that she would never get the funds for the refurbishment from Congress, so she turned to private donors who could provide both the funds and the items needed to accomplish the task. From the first, she opposed anything approaching a campaign for indiscriminate gifts. She formed two committees. One, headed by antiques expert Henry F. du Pont, was charged with deciding if a piece was appropriate to a specific room in the White House. The other, under the direction of James W. Fosburgh, was charged with soliciting gifts of art and deciding which donations should be accepted.

To supplement the collection of funds, a guidebook to the White House was published with all profits going to the underwriting of the restoration. More than one million copies were sold.

The finest existing portrait of John James Audubon was bought. A rare bronze by Frederick Remington was given as a gift from Fort Worth, Texas. Publisher Walter H. Annenberg contributed a 1767 portrait of Benjamin Franklin. All three of the so-called public rooms—designated as the Green, the Blue, and the Red Rooms—were completely refurbished.

To maintain the integrity of the Kennedy restoration, the White House was designated a national monument with museum status under the administration of the National Park Service. It was the first time the furniture, paintings, and memorabilia of the president's home were given any kind of protection. The only relocation of White House property allowed would be its reassignment to the Smithsonian Institution.

The impact of Jacqueline Kennedy was not limited to the renovation of the White House. During her short residency, the number of visitors to the mansion on Pennsylvania Avenue more than doubled during the twelve-month period following her broadcast. Thus it was appropriate that the woman who served as the nation's tour guide to the White House should become the first and only first lady to receive an Emmy award.

As great as her role was in the televised tour of the White House, her lasting image in the national conscience is also one that was brought into millions of homes across the country and around the world by television—that of a grieving widow who supervised the three days of mourning between the death and burial of her husband following his assassination in Dallas in November 1963.

21

From Martha to Hillary

Notable and Not-So-Notable Firsts

One of a Kind

Vivacious Dolley Madison, who was charming without being beautiful, is the only mistress of the White House to use snuff in public.

Except for Eliza Johnson, no first lady has kept Jersey cows on the White House lawn as a source of milk.

Mary Todd Lincoln is the only wife of a president to be legally committed to a mental institution.

Only Abigail Adams was both wife and mother of a president—John and John Quincy Adams.

Only Anna Harrison was both wife and grandmother of a president—William Henry and Benjamin.

Only one divorced wife of a future president, Ronald Reagan, won an Academy Award: Jane Wyman for her performance in *Johnny Belinda* (1948).

Only one mistress of the White House appeared in ten motion pictures: Nancy Reagan (during the period 1949–59).

Mary Todd Lincoln was probably the most controversial first lady in American history. It surprised almost no one when she was committed briefly to a sanitarium. [BRADY STUDIO, LIBRARY OF CONGRESS]

Hillary Rodham Clinton is the only first lady whose pre-Washington take-home pay greatly exceeded her husband's salary.

Bess Truman holds the record for living past age ninety-five.

Pomp and Circumstance

The only first lady to serve as U.S. ambassador to the United Nations was Eleanor Roosevelt.

Dolley Madison was the only assignee of a reserved seat of honor in the gallery of the House of Representatives.

As Lucy Ware Webb, the future wife of Rutherford B. Hayes was the first to earn a college degree, receiving it from Ohio Wesleyan Female College in Cincinnati.

Grace Goodhue Coolidge was the first to receive an honorary academic degree, an LL.D. from Boston University (she quipped that it ought to have been a D.D.—Doctor of Domesticity).

At the 1968 Republican National Convention in Miami, Nancy Reagan applauds upon hearing that her husband will be a candidate for the presidency. [ASSOCIATED PRESS]

Lady Bird Johnson was first to be hostess of a formal dinner given in the Rose Garden.

Jacqueline Bouvier Kennedy received the only Special Emmy Award, for arranging a televised tour of the White House.

Of Time and Space

All signs of the Zodiac are represented by one, two, three, or more first ladies:

Aries (March 21–April 19)
Lou Henry Hoover (March 29, 1875)
Elizabeth Ann Bloomer Warren Ford (April 18, 1918)
Lucretia Rudolph Garfield (April 19, 1832)
Taurus (April 20–May 20)
Julia Gardiner Tyler (May 4, 1820)
Ellen Louise Axson Wilson (May 15, 1860)
Dorothea (Dolley) Todd Payne Madison (May 20, 1768)

Gemini (May 21–June 21)
Ida Saxton McKinley (June 8, 1847)
Barbara Pierce Bush (June 8, 1924)
Anne Frances (Nancy) Robbins Davis Reagan (July 6, 1921)

Cancer (June 22–July 22)
Martha Dandridge Custis Washington (June 21, 1731)
Elizabeth Kortright Monroe (June 30, 1768)
Frances Folsom Cleveland (July 21, 1864)

Leo (July 23–August 22)
Anna Tuthill Harrison (July 25, 1775)
Jacqueline Lee Bouvier Kennedy (July 28, 1929)
Edith Kermit Carow Roosevelt (August 6, 1861)
Florence Mabel Kling De Wolfe Harding (August 15, 1860)
Eleanor Rosalynn Smith Carter (August 18, 1927)

Virgo (August 23–September 22)
Lucy Ware Webb Hayes (August 28, 1831)
Helen Herron Taft (September 2, 1861)
Sarah Childress Polk (September 4, 1803)
Margaret Mackall Smith Taylor (September 21, 1788)

Libra (September 23–October 23)
Eliza McCardle Johnson (October 4, 1810)
Caroline Lavinia Scott Harrison (October 10, 1832)
Anna Eleanor Roosevelt (October 11, 1884)
Edith Bolling Galt Wilson (October 15, 1872)

Scorpio (October 24–November 21)
Hillary Rodham Clinton (October 26, 1948)
Letitia Christian Tyler (November 12, 1790)
Mamie Geneva Doud Eisenhower (November 14, 1896)

Sagittarius (November 22–December 21)
Abigail Smith Adams (November 22, 1744)
Claudia Alta Taylor Johnson (December 12, 1912)
Mary Ann Todd Lincoln (December 13, 1818)

Capricorn (December 22–January 19)
Grace Anna Goodhue Coolidge (January 3, 1879)

Aquarius (January 20–February 18)
Julia Boggs Dent Grant (January 26, 1826)
Louisa Catherine Johnson Adams (February 12, 1775)
Elizabeth Virginia Wallace Truman (February 13, 1885)

Pisces (February 19–March 20)
Jane Means Appleton Pierce (March 12, 1806)

Abigail Powers Fillmore (March 13, 1798)
Thelma Catherine (Patricia) Ryan Nixon (March 16, 1912)

Several states have produced more than their share of first ladies.
Hence only eighteen of fifty can claim to have been birthplaces to
the wives of the presidents:

Connecticut
Edith Kermit Carow Roosevelt (Norwich)
Georgia
Ellen Louise Axson Wilson (Savannah)
Eleanor Rosalynn Smith Carter (Plains)
Illinois
Elizabeth Ann Bloomer Warren Ford (Chicago)
Hillary Rodham Clinton (Chicago)
Iowa
Lou Henry Hoover (Waterloo)
Mamie Geneva Doud Eisenhower (Boone)
Kentucky
Mary Ann Todd Lincoln (Lexington)
Eliza McCardle Johnson (Leesburg)
Maryland
Margaret Mackall Smith Taylor (Calvert County)
Massachusetts
Abigail Smith Adams (Weymouth)
Missouri
Julia Boggs Dent Grant (Saint Louis)
Elizabeth Virginia Wallace Truman (Independence)
Nevada
Thelma Catherine (Patricia) Ryan Nixon (Ely)
New Hampshire
Jane Means Appleton Pierce (Hampton)
New Jersey
Anna Tuthill Harrison (Morristown)
New York
Elizabeth Kortright Monroe (New York)
Julia Gardiner Tyler (Gardiner's Island)
Abigail Powers Fillmore (Stillwater)
Frances Folsom Cleveland (Buffalo)
Anna Eleanor Roosevelt (New York)

Jacqueline Lee Bouvier Kennedy (Southampton)
Anne Frances (Nancy) Robbins Davis Reagan (New York)
Barbara Pierce Bush (Rye)
North Carolina
Dorothea (Dolley) Todd Payne Madison (Guilford County)
Ohio
Lucy Ware Webb Hayes (Chillicothe)
Lucretia Rudolph Garfield (Garretsville)
Caroline Lavinia Scott Harrison (Oxford)
Ida Saxton McKinley (Canton)
Helen Herron Taft (Cincinnati)
Florence Mabel Kling De Wolfe Harding (Marion)
Tennessee
Sarah Childress Polk (Rutherford County)
Texas
Claudia Alta Taylor Johnson (Karnack)
Vermont
Grace Anna Goodhue Coolidge (Burlington)
Virginia
Martha Dandridge Custis Washington (New Kent County)
Letitia Christian Tyler (New Kent County)
Edith Bolling Galt Wilson (Wytheville)
Overseas
Louisa Catherine Johnson Adams (London, England)

Service Above All

Julia Tyler, who made her debut at fifteen and later married a man old enough to be her father, was the first to serve as first lady while in her twenties.

Prior to Jacqueline Kennedy, no woman performed the functions of a president's wife during her thirties.

Dolley Madison, having abandoned the Quaker gray of her girlhood, was first to serve as mistress of the President's Mansion while in her forties.

Florence Harding was first to serve as the first lady of the United States during her sixties.

Frances Cleveland, who had been the ward of Grover Cleveland, was the first woman to serve two nonconsecutive terms as first lady. She was also the only first lady to be married in the White House.

Sarah Polk served as private secretary to her husband during his presidency.

Rosalynn Carter was the first spouse of a chief executive to regularly attend cabinet meetings.

Trail Blazers

Anna Harrison was the first widow of a president to receive a sort of pension. When her husband died after only one month in office, Congress sent her twenty-five thousand dollars—the salary he would have drawn during the first year of his term of office had he lived.

Until Lou Hoover, no first lady had delivered a radio address.

Wives of the first eight presidents had one thing in common: not one of them regularly attended a school during girlhood. Thus Anna Harrison was the first formally educated first lady—her prosperous grandparents saw to it that she seldom missed a day of school.

Lou Hoover was the first first lady with an earned graduate degree. She had prepared for a professional career in geology at Stanford University.

In 1916 Edith Wilson broke ranks with her predecessors by purchasing American-made china for use at White House dinners.

While some of her predecessors gave occasional interviews to news reporters, Eleanor Roosevelt was the first first lady to hold a formal press conference.

Ignoring more than a century of tradition, Helen Taft was the first mistress of the White House to furnish one of its bedrooms with twin beds.

Florence Harding was the first first lady to vote for her husband for president.

Edith Wilson was the first to stock the White House with American-made china.

Eleanor Roosevelt was the first mistress of the White House to appear as a character in a novel (Elliott Roosevelt's *Murder and the First Lady*).

First Mothers

When Anna Harrison's tenth child was born, no other first lady had been the mother of ten living children.

Frances Cleveland was the first mistress of the White House to give birth to a child in the mansion, daughter Esther in 1893.

While John Quincy Adams was serving as U.S. ambassador to Russia, his wife Louisa gave birth to the first child of a first lady to be born outside the United States. Unfortunately, the infant, a daughter, survived for only a year and died in 1811.

Last of All . . .

Not long after leaving the White House, William Howard Taft became chief justice of the U.S. Supreme Court and thus remained

Helen Taft was the first first lady to be buried in Arlington National Cemetery.

in Washington, D.C. His wife, Helen, is buried beside him, the only first lady interred in Arlington National Cemetery.

Edith Wilson, widow of Woodrow Wilson, is the only first lady to die on her husband's birthday.

Mary Todd Lincoln, a Kentucky belle transformed into a woman of many woes, was the first to see one of her children die in the Executive Mansion. Her son William Wallace, age twelve, fell seriously ill in February 1862 with what doctors diagnosed as "bilious fever." Willie's death is believed to have been brought about by typhoid fever, contracted from drinking Potomac River water pumped into the mansion.

Despite the fact that the Kentucky-born Civil War mistress of the Executive Mansion was suspected of being a Southern sympathizer, she was never questioned by a congressional investigating body. Such action was unthinkable in the 1860s. Not so in the 1990s when Hillary Rodham Clinton had the dubious distinction of being first to be formally questioned by a special counsel investigating a failed Clinton financial deal.

Part 4

First Lady Challenges and Controversies

*Jane Pierce, a reluctant first lady, doted on her only surviving son, Bennie.
Her first child had lived only a few days, and her second had died of typhus at
age four.*

22

Jane Pierce

Death Rode the Rails

Dear Mamma, Edward brought the news from Boston that Father is a candidate for the presidency. I hope he won't be elected for I should not like to be at Washington and I think you would not either.—Bennie"

Born on April 13, 1841, Bennie was more than "the apple of his mother's eye." Her life revolved around him, partly because she had lost two other children.

Jane Means Appleton Pierce's oldest child, Franklin, died shortly after his birth, possibly the victim of what is today called sudden infant death syndrome. Frank Robert, her second son, died suddenly at the age of four from typhus. Now Bennie, regarded by his mother as precocious, was approaching his tenth birthday and had experienced no serious illness.

His plaintive little letter, scribbled on note paper and dispatched from his home in Concord, New Hampshire, to Boston, clearly reflected his mother's attitude. Described as "shy and retiring," these qualities may have developed as a result of her fragile health. One account states that she was "from girlhood inclined toward being tubercular."

The daughter of a former president of Bowdoin College, she was strikingly different from Franklin Pierce, whom she met when he was a student there. The son of a two-time governor of New Hampshire, Franklin was gregarious and sociable. One of his close friends was Nathaniel Hawthorne.

Upon graduation, he began to practice law in Concord but became interested in politics, starting in the New Hampshire legislature and moving to the U.S. House of Representatives. What attracted Jane and Franklin to one another was an enigma to their mutual acquaintances, but they were married in 1834.

Shortly after their wedding, Pierce became the youngest U.S. senator at the age of thirty-three. Jane, however, was not comfortable in Washington and despite plans on finding a suitable home in the capital, she returned to her parents' home in Amherst. Communicating her great displeasure at his absence in Washington, Franklin resigned from the Senate a year before his term was to expire and returned to his law practice in Concord.

Soon after the Mexican War began in 1846, Pierce received a colonel's commission in the U.S. Army from President James K. Polk and quickly secured a brigadier's rank with the help of Washington friends. When thrown from a horse in the attack on Churubusco, he suffered a leg injury but returned to the field the next day. There he wrenched his injured leg, fainted from the pain, and lay helpless on the field under fire until the end of the battle. Later his political opponents distorted these facts to accuse him of cowardice on the battlefield.

After the war and returning to his law practice, Pierce continued his political interests and was chairman of the New Hampshire Democratic Party when the national convention met in Baltimore to pick a presidential candidate in 1852. Jane reluctantly told her husband good-bye as he headed south. There the delegates could not agree on their choice for the nominee, so on the thirty-fifth ballot they turned to a dark horse, Franklin Pierce. Fourteen ballots later Jane Pierce's husband became his party's choice for the highest office in the land. It was this turn of events that prompted Bennie to write from his boarding school to his mother, temporarily staying in Boston with friends.

Despite the hopes of Bennie and his mother, Franklin Pierce won the presidency. During the Christmas season, Jane saw little of her husband, who was finding the selection of a cabinet more difficult than he had expected.

Since Franklin was so busy, Jane and Bennie spent the holidays at Andover and then planned to return to Concord for the winter term of Bennie's school. On January 6 the reunited family boarded a morning train for home. They were in their seats well before the conductor shouted the familiar "All aboard!" Discussing what had

Franklin Pierce retired from politics after spending thirteen years in the New Hampshire and national legislatures. Ten years after he had resumed his law practice, he received his party's nomination for the presidency. Jane Pierce fainted when she heard he had accepted it. [BRADY STUDIO, NATIONAL ARCHIVES]

taken place during their period of separation, Franklin was listening to an account of a Christmas dinner when their car "seemed almost to be jolted into the air."

Seconds later there was a loud snap, sounding much like the breaking of metal. It was still ringing in their ears when the car in which they rode was thrown from the tracks. Toppling down an embankment, it somehow stayed nearly upright as it rolled into a farmer's field. Authorities never explained the cause of the accident. Their official report noted with satisfaction that "despite the severity of the crash, there was only one casualty."

That casualty was Bennie Pierce, whose body was broken and mangled. A few days later, the town of Concord mourned as twelve fellow students served as pallbearers at his funeral. Friends noted that "Jane was clearly still in the depths of shock; her eyes were glazed, and she appeared not to recognize old acquaintances."

As days passed, the grief of the mother who lost her only remaining child became deeper. She told her husband, "The wreck was an act of God. God decided to take our precious little boy, so that you will have no distractions as you set out to effect reconciliation between sections of our nation."

After Bennie's death, Jane Pierce was in perpetual mourning. She asked her aunt, Abby Kent Means, and the wife of the secretary of war, Varina Davis, to act as White House hostesses in her stead.
[J. C. BUTTRE ENGRAVING]

Soon the tenor of Jane's remarks underwent radical change. God had little or nothing to do with Bennie's death, she declared. It was the direct result of her husband's political ambitions, she told him repeatedly.

Dismayed, Franklin Pierce at last spoke out. "Bennie is gone," he said. "Nothing that we do can bring him back. Voters of the United States have registered their preference that I serve them as president. That means I cannot and must not defer my official duties any longer."

Leaving Jane in Concord, Franklin suffered through his inauguration. No preparations had been made for the arrival of the new first family, so the president and a lone aide groped through a disordered mansion until they found bedrooms where they spent the first few nights of his administration.

Jane reluctantly took up residence in the Executive Mansion a few weeks later, but she made it clear that she was not happy there and never expected to be. During the first half of the Pierce administration, she remained secluded in her upstairs bedroom. She read her Bible daily, but her chief occupation was writing letters to Bennie, a wisp of whose hair she carried in a locket. Washingtonians called her "the shadow of the White House." Finally on January 1, 1855, she attended a state dinner, where she was described as "the very picture of melancholy."

For ninety-pound Jane Pierce, life effectively ended with sudden death upon the rails in January 1853. No other first lady was so preoccupied with the past and disdainful of her role.

When Franklin Pierce lost the election of 1856 to James Buchanan, he and Jane traveled abroad for two years to try to restore her health. They returned with several crates of paintings and souvenirs to embellish their Concord home, but Jane's memories of Benny and the house were too much for her, and they moved to Andover.

Inevitably, Franklin Pierce returned to politics and criticized all actions leading up to and including the Civil War until he had no remaining political friends. Jane gradually lost all interest in the world and her health began to fail. She died in Andover, Massachusetts, on December 2, 1863.

23

Dolley Madison

Matchmaker

Shall I again that Harp unstring
Which long hath been a useless thing,
Unheard in Lady's bower?
Its notes were once full wild and free,
When I, to one as fair as thee,
Did sing in youth's bright hours.
Like to those raven tresses, gay,
Which o'er thy ivory shoulders play,
Were those which waked my lyre.

*J*ohn Tyler, six feet tall and noted as the first man to become chief executive because of a president's death in office, was shyly proud. He had not written a poem for many years; now he had what he considered to be a gem.

On March 8, 1843, he penned all twenty-one of his lines in an autograph album belonging to the daughter of a New York state senator. Julia Gardiner, who said she wanted a few more autographs before Congress adjourned, waved to Henry Baldwin a few days later.

"Do place your autograph in my album, please!" she began.

"Certainly, young lady. What's more, I'll put it under my arm and carry it for you; both of us seem to be headed toward Capitol Hill."

Julia relinquished the ornately decorated album—complete with the Tyler poem in its pages—and Baldwin thumbed through it before adding his message and signature. Soon official Washington was buzzing with talk about "Tyler's romantic ideas expressed in iambic tetrameter verse."

No doubt about it: Recently having lost his wife of thirty years, Tyler was smitten by the raven-haired beauty from the North. He became acquainted with her soon after David Gardiner and his family moved to Washington from Long Island. Within a few months after they met, the president took every opportunity to let Julia know that he had eyes only for her.

Julia was far less enthusiastic about a romantic involvement. Earlier she had rejected three suitors in quick succession. She never met Letitia Christian Tyler, who functioned as first lady from 1841 to 1842. Perhaps she would have liked her, but she did not like the idea of being compared with her in a tedious and rambling poem. To complicate matters, she was far from sure that she could develop "a suitable interest" in a man old enough to be her father.

Sensing that an impasse was in the making, the dowager queen of Washington society decided to take a hand in the matter. Dolley Madison, whose eight years in the President's House were marked by splendid entertainment, had returned to the capital after the death of her husband.

Earlier noted for her role in saving a Gilbert Stuart portrait of George Washington when the British burned what is now the White House, the widow Madison had lost none of her earlier charm. She attracted all eyes whenever she entered a ballroom wearing a low-cut bodice and a Turkish turban—her standard attire on fashionable occasions.

When fur magnate John Jacob Astor laid eyes on Dolley, he was so intrigued that he inquired about her financial background. Soon he discovered that despite her lavish dinners and expensive gowns she was all but impoverished. As a result Astor bought the mortgage on her home at Sixteenth and H Streets and refused to accept more than token rent from her.

Astor's tribute was one of hundreds that were paid to the vivacious native of North Carolina during her long reign over society in the nation's capital. No important Washington festivity was complete unless Dolley attended. She took part in ceremonies that launched the building of the Washington Monument and regularly occupied the special seat in the visitors gallery reserved for her by the House of Representatives.

Dolley Madison was a trendsetter in Washington fashion and adopted the Turkish turban for everyday use. She remained the grand dame of the capital until her death at age eighty-one. [NEW YORK HISTORICAL SOCIETY]

Soon after having planned the nation's first inaugural ball in 1809 she presided over the first wedding held in the President's House. In a gala ceremony her widowed sister became the bride of Thomas Todd, an associate justice of the U.S. Supreme Court. When a son of Martin Van Buren indicated romantic interest in her cousin, she planned and directed the wedding of Angelica Singleton. If anyone could advance the romantic interests of Tyler, Dolley was just the person to do so.

Later in the year after which Tyler had resorted to verse to express his admiration for Julia Gardiner, special invitations were issued to a cruise on the world's first screw-propeller-driven warship. John Ericsson, remembered as the inventor of the Civil War ironclad *Monitor,* had designed the USS *Princeton.* Como. Robert E. Stockton, who commanded the vessel, wanted it outfitted with the largest naval armaments available. English artisans constructed a twelve-inch wrought-iron cannon whose ammunition weighed 216 pounds. Dubbed the Oregon, it was so heavy the *Princeton* tilted a trifle when the weapon was mounted.

To balance the *Princeton,* Stockton designed another weapon of about the same weight but "substantially more powerful." When his Peacemaker cannon was mounted, the vessel rode a bit low in the water but with an even keel. Guests on the planned excursion would be privileged to demonstration firings of the world's most powerful cannon, Commodore Stockton promised.

When she learned of the cruise, Dolley Madison saw the opportunity she had been seeking. Julia was already the toast of Saratoga, New York, and was rapidly conquering Washington. Dolley would make sure that on this romantic and historic occasion Julia would see President John Tyler as a man in command.

Aboard the warship, the 150 guests enjoyed a feast that included some European dishes introduced to America by Dolley. Then, because so many people were present, they were divided into two groups to witness the firing of the Peacemaker. Below deck, civilian and military leaders shook the hand of the president and congratulated him on having elevated the United States into the rank of a world-class maritime power.

As those on deck caught a glimpse of Mount Vernon, someone had an inspiration. "Fire the Peacemaker once more in honor of George Washington!" he cried. Stockton agreed and signaled the gunners back to their firing stations. Dolley is said to have kept Tyler below to hear her account of the first Easter egg rolling on the Capitol grounds.

When the Peacemaker was fired, the gun itself exploded, hurling fragments in every direction. David Gardiner died without visible injury; his watch stopped at 4:06. Como. Beverly Kennon, chief of naval construction, was also killed and horribly mangled. Other casualties included Secretary of State Abel P. Upshur, Secretary of the Navy Thomas W. Gilmer, two sailors, and Tyler's black body servant.

When Julia learned that her father was a victim of the explosion, she wilted to the floor of the wardroom whose punch bowls were nearly emptied by the lurching of the warship. Tyler pushed some people aside to reach her and cradle her in his arms.

Soon another vessel was alongside the stricken warship. With Julia in his arms, Tyler strode across the gangplank and directed the captain of the rescue vessel to proceed toward the President's House. By the time she was beginning to recover, Julia found herself in one of the bedrooms of the mansion, where she spent the night.

Dolley wept openly at the loss of life on that fateful afternoon, but her eyes glistened when she told intimates how Tyler had

When the heavy gun known as the Peacemaker was fired for the third time, it exploded and killed six people, including Sen. David Gardiner of New York.
[CURRIER & IVES LITHOGRAPH]

responded to the crisis. "Had I planned every detail, it could not have come off better," she often said.

On June 26, 1844, four months after Tyler carried Julia from the shattered *Princeton,* they became husband and wife in a secret New York ceremony. As twenty-four-year-old Julia said "I do" in response to a question by the Reverend Gregory T. Bedell, she looked lovingly into the eyes of her fifty-four-year-old bridegroom.

Perhaps they would have married had Dolley not finagled for them to be together at a time when Tyler might make a powerful impression. Nevertheless, the dowager queen of Washington reveled in having played the role of matchmaker and having had a hand in the first marriage of a sitting president.

"I had some small part in elevating a girl in her twenties into the ranks of us old ladies who remember our own days as first lady," she sometimes remarked with a twinkle.

24

Julia Grant

A Gala Cover-up

Chewing on an unlighted cigar, a sure sign of tension, Ulysses S. Grant summarized the most important matter on his mind.

"Hayes and some of his family arrived here soon after nine this morning. There's no way to keep it a secret; the *Sun* says a crowd of more than two thousand were on hand to greet them."

"Under the circumstances, I guess I'm surprised," Julia Grant confessed.

"Shouldn't be; the Democrats have been promising trouble. Everybody in the country knows that March 4 comes on Sunday this year, so ceremonies are planned for Monday. That gives the opposition plenty of time to stir up trouble."

"Hasn't inauguration day fallen on Sunday before?"

Grant nodded. "At least twice; Madison and Taylor both took the oath a day late. But times were different then. Neither of them was accused of having stolen the election."

"This 'stolen election' business is nonsense," Julia exploded. "You've seen to it that everything was done in proper order."

"Sure, but the new electoral commission ran into trouble as soon as it was created. Starting with the first time they met in January they've been hounded by a bunch of reporters. That's the real reason they didn't announce a decision until 2 A.M. today. By that time, Hayes was already on the train and it was too late to advise him to wait until Monday to come."

"What about Tilden?"

"Don't know. If he's here, he's lying low," the president said. "Wouldn't put it past the Democrats to have the hotels packed with squads of their rowdies, waiting to try to get the Bible into Tilden's hand Monday morning.

"Met with aides late this afternoon; some of them think we ought to have the ceremony on Sunday."

"Would that keep the Democrats from making a commotion that could turn ugly in a hurry?" Julia wondered.

"Not if they did not know what was going on," her husband admitted.

"Then you ought to have a secret ceremony on Sunday; after all, that's the official date of the inauguration."

"You're a lot of help!" Grant grunted. "Sounds good, but how on earth can you keep old Washington hands from spotting Hayes and the chief justice?"

"Give me a few minutes to think," Julia Grant requested. "I may be able to come up with a suggestion."

After ten minutes of silence the first lady proposed that they invite a few officials, friends, and members of their families to dinner on Sunday evening. "You can get sailors from the naval base to deliver the invitations," she pointed out. "That way, they won't be spotted as White House messengers."

Grant, famous for making quick battlefield decisions and sticking to them, nodded vigorously. "Go ahead," he directed. "Better keep the guest list under fifty.

"No need to use sailors to deliver invitations, though," he decided. "Let the newspapers know that we plan to make our last dinner here something out of the ordinary. . . . You can think of something. Instead of trying to keep it quiet, the more publicity we get, the better it will be."

The never-before-encountered dilemma of the Grants—and the nation—grew out of a unique presidential election in the U.S. centennial year of 1876. Blasting the Grant regime as "an era of unparalleled corruption and scandal," for the first time in twenty years Democrats sensed that they had a chance to win the White House. Republicans, in turn, charged their opponents with using force to gain votes in the South.

When ballots were counted many newspapers issued special editions hailing Democrat Samuel J. Tilden as the president-elect. John C. Reid, managing editor of the *New York Times*, took a more cautious stance. Results were being challenged in South Carolina,

To avoid any awkwardness in the transition of power to his successor, President Ulysses S. Grant adopted a plan devised by the first lady. [H. B. HALL ENGRAVING]

Oregon, Florida, and Louisiana; legal contests in these states could decide the election, he concluded.

When a special edition of the *Times* hit the streets, readers were informed that Tilden held 184 electoral votes—just one short of victory. According to the newspaper, Hayes had carried states that gave him 181 votes in the electoral college.

Oregon's lone electoral vote soon went to Hayes, but each of the three contested southern states sent dual slates of electors to Washington. With the electoral college clearly unable to proceed as usual, Congress appointed a fifteen-member commission to decide which electoral votes should go to Hayes and which to Tilden. Seven known Republicans, seven known Democrats, and one independent—David Davis of Illinois—made up the body.

Under intense pressure, Davis took the easy way out and resigned from the commission. Joseph Bradley of New Jersey, an outspoken Republican, was named to fill the vacancy.

During day after day of heated argument the special electoral commission took one vote after another. Always, the result was eight votes for Hayes, seven for Tilden. Saying that a refusal to concede might lead to another civil war, the Democratic candidate asked that his name be withdrawn. Opponents denounced this as a ploy designed to prolong the work of the commission and make possible a last-minute coup by members of his party.

Although mocked by cartoonist Thomas Nast, Samuel Tilden yielded the White House rather than risk another civil war. [HARPER'S WEEKLY]

It was in this climate that Julia Grant—who earlier had fervently hoped to see her husband win a third term in the White House— invited her guests for a "Sunday evening dinner," to "pay their compliments to President-elect and Mrs. Hayes."

When the guests arrived on March 4, 1876, they were ushered into the East Room "to see President Grant and the first lady once more." Then they were directed, "instead of taking the arms of husbands, ladies will be escorted by their eldest sons." This resulted in considerable commotion, after which the cream of Washington society walked through a hall to the dining room.

There is no record that a single guest was aware that the president and the president-elect eased out of the East Room while the promenade line was forming. Passing rapidly through the Blue Room and into the Red Room, they found Chief Justice Morrison R. Waite ready for them, having slipped into the mansion from the south side. Once the brief inaugural ceremony was concluded, all three men joined the dinner party. Until Monday morning no reporter knew what had taken place.

Rutherford B. Hayes became the nineteenth president of the United States by taking the oath of office in a secret ceremony.

Hayes, already president, repeated the oath of office in public on Monday to the applause of an immense crowd. At no time was there any attempt by Democrats to circumvent the electoral commission's decision or even to create a disturbance.

An unforgettable dinner party planned by Julia Grant had served as a cover for secret inaugural ceremonies with no counterpart before or since. The sadness of the former first lady at her departure from Washington was tempered by the realization that she had successfully ended the contest over "the stolen election."

25

Bess Truman

The Woman from Missouri

Mother! Mother!"

Embracing her mother as she spoke, Margaret Truman could not restrain her own tears. Normally self-contained and undemonstrative, Bess Truman was behaving in a highly unusual fashion. Before dropping the telephone into its cradle, she burst into a spasm of sobs.

After what seemed to her daughter to be an eternity, the wife of the vice president of the United States began to regain her composure. "It's the president!" she gasped. "He's dead!"

Remembering that April 1945 incident long afterward, Margaret said she understood her mother's response to the telephone call from her father. Throughout the 1944 campaign, Franklin Delano Roosevelt, the patrician from New York, had given his running mate, the senator from Missouri, no role in the campaign. Bess Truman never fully forgave him for what seemed to be a calculated insult. Her mother's reaction, Margaret realized, was not grief but the realization that she would have to assume the role of first lady.

Elizabeth Virginia Wallace, always called Bess, and Harry S. Truman first met at Sunday school in 1890 when he was six years old and she a year younger. When she tossed her golden curls above her sparkling blue eyes, an awestruck small boy was instantly smitten. From that time forward they were classmates, graduating from high school in 1901, friends, and eventually sweethearts.

158

Bess Truman was vastly different in temperament and style from her immediate predecessor, Eleanor Roosevelt. Comparisons were inevitable but unfair to the woman who treasured her privacy.

As adolescents, both Harry and Bess suffered severe traumas. Harry's father, John Truman, was bankrupted in 1901, so his son began holding down two or three part-time jobs to help put bread on the table. Two years later David W. Wallace, holder of an obscure local political office, committed suicide and his daughter never quite got over the shame of it.

Harry worked as a timekeeper for a contractor, as a mailroom clerk in a newspaper office, and then as clerk and later bookkeeper at a Kansas City bank. Each time he changed jobs, his pay increased, jumping from thirty-five dollars a month in 1901 to seventy-five dollars in 1904. He was running the family farm when America entered World War I, and he joined the 129th Field Artillery in August 1917 as a lieutenant.

Six weeks after his discharge in 1919, Major Truman married Bess and formed a partnership with an army buddy. Their Kansas City haberdashery was mildly prosperous until the recession of 1922. "I figure that my half of the store's debt is nearly thirty thousand dollars," Harry told Bess. "Bankruptcy is not my style, so we'll have to skimp and save until every penny is paid."

Winning election as a district judge—a post similar to a county commissioner in some states—Harry was soon in charge of sprawling Jackson County, Missouri. It took him and Bess twelve hard years to pay off the obligations from which a bankruptcy court would have relieved him. Their elation at finally being out of debt was still fresh when he decided to run for the U.S. Senate.

He won against an entrenched incumbent in November 1934. Fearful of the high cost of living in the nation's capital, he put Bess, whom he called "the Boss," on the payroll as his secretary at just under two hundred dollars per month. She helped him to write speeches, advised him on issues, and eventually saw her salary increase to forty-five hundred dollars a year. With the senator then earning ten thousand dollars annually, they were finally free of financial pressure.

Senator Truman developed a national reputation as chairman of a committee investigating inefficiency and waste in the government. The Truman Committee saved the nation as much as a billion dollars and increased war production during World War II.

Although he did not want the vice presidency in 1944, he yielded to pressure to become the compromise candidate. He held that important-sounding office only a few months, but that was long enough for him to become thoroughly disgusted with it. Questioned by a reporter concerning his role, he said, "A fellow holding this job finds himself about as useful as a cow's fifth teat."

After only eighty-three days into his fourth term, Roosevelt died suddenly at Warm Springs, Georgia. Frances Perkins, the secretary of labor, was one of those attending the brief White House ceremony on April 12, 1945, when Harry S. Truman became the thirty-third president of the United States. She never forgot Bess Truman's expression, she said, "swollen with tears as she contemplated the role she was about to assume."

Bess and Margaret then quickly returned to their $125-a-month apartment in a rent-controlled building on Connecticut Avenue. When the new president came home that night at 10 P.M., driving his own car, she hugged him and said, "Be sure to tell Mrs. Roosevelt that we'll stay here as long as she wishes."

Eleanor Roosevelt expressed her gratitude to Bess for her graciousness but indicated that she planned to vacate the White House immediately. "Before I go, I will make one little gesture that will help you to get started," she said. "I'll introduce you to the ladies who will be coming to your press conferences. Many of them were at my very first one, a dozen years ago."

Bess Truman's face did not reveal her inner panic as she agreed to the meeting, but she soon had second thoughts. A few days later she wrote to Ruth Montgomery, chairperson of Mrs. Roosevelt's Press Conference Association: "I do not expect to hold press conferences."

Months later, some unhappy members of the ladies' press corps assembled at the White House after having submitted a written questionnaire to the first lady. When Bess sat down, an aide passed out copies of the questions that had been submitted and answered in writing. Typical queries and responses ran: If you had been given a choice, would you have gone into the White House?—No. Do you think we will ever have a woman as president?—No. What would you and President Truman like to do when his term of office expires?—Return to Independence, Missouri.

In a personal letter, the woman from Missouri lamented, "I am not used to this awful public life." Within weeks after becoming mistress of the White House she was calling it "the Great White Jail." When a persistent reporter demanded to know how members of the press corps would ever get to know her, she retorted: "You do not need to know me; I am not the chief executive, and I have nothing to say to the public."

In January 1946, a *Newsweek* column observed: "After nine months in the White House, Mrs. Harry S Truman is little known, even in Washington. She did her Christmas shopping alone and unnoticed in department stores of the capital."

When she went shopping the first lady drove her own car. She addressed her own Christmas cards and kept a tight rein on White House expenditures. She invited her Independence bridge club to the White House for card games. Assistant usher J. B. West, who was a liaison person with other staff members, called her Sunshine "because she is always upbeat in her attitude."

The Trumans were scrupulous about finances. The president even paid for the stamps on his own mail. Bess was indignant when Saks Fifth Avenue sent her nylons and ordered an immediate end to the practice of sending gifts to the first family.

The Roosevelts had made their home in the White House for thirteen years and had seen to it that the crippled president's special needs were met. The Monroe Drawing Room had been converted into his bedroom with specially designed appointments, and

The Truman family was very happy in one another's company. The White House staff dubbed them the Three Musketeers. Bess was known for her infectious laughter, and stories circulated of watermelon seed fights and heated Ping-Pong games.

the Monroe furniture had been placed in storage. The Trumans found that they had the same latitude in decorating the house, and so Bess restored the Monroe Room to its pre-Roosevelt look, complete with the furniture that had been in storage for more than a decade. Some viewed these changes as a repudiation of the Roosevelts, but that ascribes a motive to a practice followed by most new families that came to occupy the White House.

Twelve years after her parents, King George and Queen Elizabeth, had visited the Roosevelts, their daughter, Elizabeth and her husband, Philip, paid a state visit to the White House. Bess, as usual, did her duty but did not try any innovations, such as offering hot dogs to the royal couple. After a formal state dinner, the duke of Edinburgh said, "From now on, it would be fitting for us in Britain to refer to Mrs. Truman as a second Good Queen Bess."

After Truman won a tremendous upset election and served a full term as president in his own right, the Trumans fulfilled Bess's wish and happily returned to Independence. There they settled into the big old house where Bess had been born. She resumed her place in the ladies' bridge club and outlived her husband by ten years, dying in 1982 at the age of ninety-seven, the longest living of any first lady.

26

Mary Todd Lincoln

Scandalous!

The former Mary Todd, once the belle of Lexington, Kentucky, was at her wits' end. Bedeviled with bills she could not pay and consumed with anxiety about her future, the former first lady knew only one person she could trust. Hence she sat down in her Chicago hotel room in March 1867 and addressed a plaintive letter to Elizabeth Keckley.

Born into slavery, Keckley is the only person known to have served in the households of two women whose husbands became warring presidents. After having worked a number of years for Varina Davis, she went to Washington and quickly found a place in the Executive Mansion. Mary Todd Lincoln, who knew that her new servant was intimately acquainted with the Confederate president, Jefferson Davis, never questioned Elizabeth's loyalty.

Writing to her former servant, Lincoln's widow explained that she had put all available figures on paper. Studying them, she concluded that she would have to give up her lodgings and seek an inexpensive boarding house in which to spend her remaining years. Then she announced a decision:

> It will not be startling news to you, my dear Lizzie, to learn that I must sell off a portion of my wardrobe to add to my resources. You remember what I told you in Washington; I cannot live on $1,700 a year. As I have many costly things which I shall never wear, I might as well turn them into money, and thus add to my income and make my circum-

Mary Todd Lincoln feared that as a widow she would soon be penniless. [BRADY STUDIO, LIBRARY OF CONGRESS]

stances easier. It is humiliating to be placed in such a position, but, I must extricate myself as best I can. Now, Lizzie, I want to ask a favor of you. It is imperative that I should do something for my relief, so I want you to meet me in New York between the 30th of August and the 5th of September next, to assist me in disposing of a portion of my wardrobe.

Elizabeth Keckley not only preserved that unusual letter; she included much of it in the book she published about her Washington experiences.

After exchanging several more letters, the former first lady and her former servant finalized their plans. Elizabeth, who had opened a small dressmaking shop in the capital, closed her establishment and went to New York. Arriving at the St. Denis Hotel on September 18, she inquired whether or not "a friend and companion, Mrs. Clarke" had arrived the previous day. Answered in the affirmative, she heaved a great sigh of relief that Abraham Lincoln's distraught widow had reached her destination safely.

The former first lady told her only confidant what she had already done. Purchasing a copy of the *New York Herald,* she read

Dressmaker Elizabeth Keckley served as a go-between in Mary Lincoln's dealings with New York merchants.

notices of diamond brokers and decided to use the firm of W. H. Brady and Company, 609 Broadway.

She then walked to the merchant's establishment and explained that she had jewelry to sell. A junior member of the firm, whom she knew only as Mr. Judd, was affable but said she was asking too much for the pieces she wished to sell.

A man whom she believed to be Judd's superior came up to make a separate appraisal and in doing so appeared to notice Mrs. Lincoln's name inside a ring. She snatched it from him, stuffed it into her pocket, and told him that if he wished to negotiate he should come to the St. Denis and ask for Mrs. Clarke.

Somewhat to the surprise of Elizabeth, a diamond merchant identified only as Mr. Keyes appeared early in the afternoon. Soon he admitted that he had discovered the identity of the woman seeking to become his client. Keyes examined "a large number of shawls, dresses, and fine laces," then agreed when Mary Lincoln said she found the St. Denis to be inferior. At his suggestion, the two women checked out and eventually found rooms in the Union Place Hotel.

At their new base they were visited by W. H. Brady, who volunteered that he was a Republican and was sure he could easily raise one hundred thousand dollars for Abraham Lincoln's widow.

While waiting for him to move into action, the two women took a big bundle of dresses and shawls to stores on Seventh Avenue. Merchants showed no interest in the secondhand clothing of Mrs. Clarke, and Mary Lincoln's supply of money was nearly exhausted. Brady then consented to advance six hundred dollars, so the widow of the Civil War president sent a load of goods to him in a hack.

In addition to a diamond ring, her unauthorized shipment included "four camels' hair shawls, one lace dress and shawl, a parasol cover, two dress patterns, and some furs." In a memorandum to Brady, Mary Lincoln said that once the items were appraised she would be willing to negotiate a sale.

When a week passed without a response, she notified him that her goods were valued at "over $24,000," but said she would sacrifice them for just $16,000.

Brady not only revealed the identity of his would-be client, he showed several of her letters to friends. When Lincoln's widow learned what had taken place, she authorized Brady to put her wardrobe on exhibition and to publish her letters to him in the *New York World*. She believed that once political backers of her husband learned of her plight, they would rush to her aid.

According to the *New York Evening Express*, throngs of women and some men came to see "Mrs. Lincoln's secondhand clothing." They came out of curiosity, however, and showed no interest in making purchases. Two dozen dresses, "folded or tossed about by frequent examinations," were described by the newspaper as exhibited upon a closed piano. Furs, laces, and jewelry were in a glass case, while "shawls rich and rare" were displayed on the backs of chairs.

Although a majority of New Yorkers laughed at the goings-on of the former first lady, a few were sympathetic. Some men "opened a subscription book" at Brady's office and suggested that everyone who came to look at her goods should contribute one dollar.

In desperation, Keckley turned to members of her own race and tried to get noted orator Frederick Douglass to give a series of lectures for her friend's benefit. Writing from Rochester in October, he repeated earlier assurances of personal interest but said he doubted that lectures at the Cooper Institute would serve the purpose intended.

Brady eventually sold four diamond rings, a set of furs, four shawls, and two dresses. His fee for services rendered was $820, which Mary Lincoln paid by check after returning to Chicago. In March 1868 he returned unsold items to his client, along with "an invoice of articles sent" which read:

1 Trunk
1 Lace dress
1 Lace dress, flounced
5 Lace shawls
3 Camel hair shawls
1 Lace parasol cover
1 Lace handkerchief
1 Sable boa
1 White boa
1 Set furs
2 Paisley shawls
2 Gold bracelets
16 Dresses
2 Opera cloaks
1 Purple shawl
1 Feather cape
28 yds. silk

When word of what had taken place in New York spread into the nation at large, Mary Lincoln became a subject of coarse jokes. It served her right, many newspaper editors told their readers, that her "old clothes sale" was an abject failure. To many it seemed just one step short of sacrilege to try to sell things that had at least tenuous ties with Abraham Lincoln. "Scandalous" became the dominant descriptive term for her attempt to lessen the "mountain of debt" Mary Lincoln had accumulated as a result of extravagant purchases.

Eventually an inventory of Lincoln's estate was made public. Just as his widow feared, loans of more than $4,000 had not been paid. Yet David Davis, executor of the estate, listed liquid assets of $79,482.70, three small tracts of real estate in Illinois, and 160 acres in Iowa. One-third of the total went to Mary Lincoln.

Although her so-called scandalous actions in New York may have tarnished the reputation of Mary Todd Lincoln, her reputation was further darkened when some years later, in 1875, her son, Robert Todd Lincoln, then a successful Chicago attorney, had her declared legally insane and committed to a sanitarium. Although the insanity verdict was overturned by another judge after four months, her reputation never recovered.

Although eccentric, a nuisance, and a compulsive shopper, many historians believe that Mary Todd Lincoln was not insane. Nevertheless, while polls consistently rank Abraham Lincoln at or near the top among "most competent and respected chief executives," Mary Todd Lincoln is always at or near the bottom in public perception of "most effective and admired first ladies."

27

Mamie Eisenhower

Target of the Tabloids

W hat do you have there, Mamie?"

"Nothing of any importance," replied the wife of the man both the Republican and Democratic Parties had tried to draft for the presidential nomination in 1948. Now in 1952 Republican demands had grown too strong to resist. Ike and Mamie Eisenhower were in their Chicago hotel room shortly before he would be nominated for president at the party's national convention.

While the room was adequate, it had few hiding places. Mamie's attempt to shove a folded newspaper under a sofa pillow had not gone unnoticed.

"If it's nothing, let me see it."

Wordless, she relinquished a tabloid whose front page blazed with the headline: WIFE OF GOP HOPEFUL A LUSH.

The retired general of the army was accustomed to challenges. He had headed all Allied European forces in World War II, directing the D-Day invasion, served as President Truman's army chief of staff, been president of Columbia University, and headed all NATO forces as supreme commander. The headline about his wife was a different matter.

His wife of thirty-six years whom he had taken to the altar at age twenty-six was being branded an alcoholic! Stunned, Eisenhower scanned the account as phrases seemed to jump from the page: "she was seen staggering . . . a habitual party-goer . . . a friend prevented her from falling . . . a big liability to the candidate . . ."

"When you were in North Africa and then England," Mamie explained, "and I was living in a Washington hotel, I had very little to do, so I went out a lot. You know how much I enjoy card parties with my friends. Plenty of drinks were always around, and a few times I guess I took one too many. When I got a warning, I quit cold turkey. Oh, I don't mean that I never touch the stuff. But I always stopped with one drink—no more. That's all there was to it, until gossip columnists began saying that I drank too much. Once the tale got started, there seemed to be no stopping it."

Eisenhower put his fingers to her lips. "Hush!" he said, quickly moving to embrace her. "I don't want to hear any more about it, ever! Now we have to hurry to the convention."

Later Mamie felt mixed emotions. She was happy that the light of her life, the only man she ever loved, would be running with Richard Nixon for the presidency against Adlai Stevenson, but she dreaded the actual campaign. Even more, she disliked the prospect of becoming mistress of the White House.

The daughter of a successful meatpacker, Mamie Geneva Doud grew up without knowing what it meant to need money. In Denver she took dancing from the exclusive Miss Hayden and graduated from the Wollcott School for Girls.

Marriage to a first lieutenant in the U.S. Army was not in the back of her mind when she went with her parents to San Antonio during the winter of 1915–16. There one of her father's friends at Fort Sam Houston introduced her to Lt. Dwight David Eisenhower, and for both of them it was love at first sight. The officer known to his friends simply as Ike had a jeweler make a replica of his West Point class ring. When Mamie nodded yes to his Valentine's Day proposal, he slipped the ring on her finger and they decided to marry soon in Denver.

A junior officer's wife, Mamie soon learned to cope as they moved from one post to another. Always congenial and outgoing, the petite young woman who was barely an inch over five feet tall was able to make what she called "instant friends."

Like many other army wives who congregated in officers' clubs, Mamie spent much of her time playing canasta, Ma-Jongg, or bridge. Accustomed to casual and moderate use of alcohol, she readily admitted that she thoroughly enjoyed a drink.

At intervals during the 1952 campaign, Mamie's speech was sometimes a bit slurred. Occasionally she complained of dizziness

In 1952, Mamie Eisenhower hit the campaign trail with her husband. [ASSOCIATED PRESS]

but usually seemed to feel better after taking motion-sickness medication and resting.

She reached an emotional high when Ike received almost thirty-four million votes, more than any previous presidential candidate. He had also outdistanced Stevenson by almost ten million votes.

During eight years in the White House, the wife of the thirty-fourth president was scrupulous in overseeing the household. Although she held no press conferences and made no speeches, she performed her social duties admirably. Nevertheless, the same old stories continued to surface. The White House chief usher, J. B. West, and Mamie's social secretary, Mary Jane McCaffree, carefully destroyed any magazine or newspaper articles that hinted that the first lady was an alcoholic.

After Ike suffered a heart attack in 1955, Mamie confided in a physician's wife with whom she had made friends. One morning her friend's husband surprised her by asking her to stop by his office in the hospital. Questioned about her health, the first lady called it "generally extremely good," but she admitted that she was subject to sudden attacks of dizziness. They usually began without warning, she said, sometimes lasting only a few minutes but sometimes persisting for two or three hours.

Whether brief or lengthy, such an episode was usually followed by sweating and nausea.

The doctor frowned as he listened to the list of symptoms, then he said, "You have all the symptoms of Ménière's syndrome." He explained that it could be extremely annoying and had no known cure, but it was not life-threatening.

Dr. W. N. Sterrett later made a formal diagnosis. Mamie was indeed a sufferer from an inner-ear condition that afflicts at least five million Americans.

Mamie Eisenhower felt relieved. "A person with Ménière's syndrome sometimes acts very much like a drunk!" she exclaimed. "Vertigo can cause you to stumble around as though you were tanked!"

Although the doctor's diagnosis appeared in a limited number of media, the announcement had no effect upon the tabloids. Until long after her death on November 1, 1979, the first lady widely remembered for her bangs and her love for the color "Mamie pink" was the subject of stories about her alleged inability to turn down "just one more little drink."

Mamie never knew it, but during the past decade some physicians have concluded that she and the famous Dutch artist Vincent Van Gogh suffered from the same ailment. Until recent years the impressionistic artist was considered to have been insane during his last years."

Ménière's syndrome typically affects only one ear and can be accompanied by tinnitus, or "ringing of the ears." Driven mad by what seems to be an incessant tolling of bells inside the head, a person like Van Gogh could be driven to slash off the ear that seemed to be the source of the agony.

In life, Mamie Eisenhower was more tormented by the gossip than by the syndrome. She died of a cardiac arrest two weeks prior to her eighty-third birthday. Her grave in Abilene, Kansas, is a national historic shrine. The first lady who was sometimes unsteady on her feet shares that honor with only one other wife of a president, Abigail Adams.

28

Nancy Reagan

She Ran with a Halter

𝒜 newspaper story is comparing you with Rosalynn Carter," an aide in the East Wing of the White House informed Nancy Reagan in January 1981.

"That's impossible," retorted the thirty-second first lady. Reflecting, she turned back and demanded, "In what way?"

"It says your inaugural outfit cost the president thirty thousand dollars and that Mrs. Carter's cost around three hundred dollars."

"Maybe," conceded Ronald Reagan's petite five-foot-four-inch wife. "She looked dowdy enough; I've heard that she made some of her things herself, on an old sewing machine."

Waving her hand to dismiss the subject, Nancy Reagan directed that her social secretary should report to her immediately.

Although her predecessor as mistress of the White House occupied little of Nancy's attention, she soon found herself in vicarious contact with Rosalynn's daughter, Amy. No other small girl had moved into the White House with her parents in many years; in 1977 there seemed to be no suitable bedroom for the six-year-old from Georgia.

Eventually "Amy's Room" became a special place within the mansion. About ten feet wide and fifteen feet long, it was an appropriate haven for a small girl. Nancy Reagan had every reminder of the room's tenant removed, converting it into a walk-in closet. When the job was completed, it was Nancy's Room instead of Amy's. One of the carpenters reported that he had worked in several mansions but

Whether selecting a designer gown or a set of tableware, Nancy Reagan wanted nothing but the best.

had never before seen "forty feet of hanging space in a single room." Housed there now were gowns, coats, and accessories, each displaying a label showing when it was last worn.

Eight years later after the Reagan administration ended, members of the housekeeping staff of the White House went public. According to them, Nancy's Room bulged with hundreds of outfits, many of them bearing the labels of famous designers. "Thousand-dollar dresses were packed in that room like sardines in a can," one staffer recalled. That verdict concerning the number of outfits may have been accurate, but the estimate of their value was too conservative by far.

In October 1988, shortly before the Reagan years were over, *Time* magazine ran a story called "Why Mrs. Reagan Still Looks Like a Million." Chris Blazakis, earlier a vice president of a firm operated by designer James Galanos, had been given a collection of photographs of the first lady taken over a period of more than five years. The fashion expert's task was to identify the maker of many of the garments she wore.

It is unlikely that Blazakis saw every costume worn by Nancy Reagan during the years in which the national debt was shooting upward at the speed of the space shuttle. Yet from the scores of photos that were examined, he estimated for *Time* that the collective value of the outfits shown in them easily exceeded one million dollars—jewelry not included. Had the husband of the first lady paid for the clothing shown, most of his salary of two hundred thousand dollars per year would have gone for this purpose.

While the president surely must have footed the bill for an occasional gown or scarf or pair of shoes, he did not spend a dime for a Galanos original whose estimated worth was more than twenty thousand dollars. Ronald Reagan did not pay a nickel for an outfit by Cuban-born designer Adolfo that would have cost any other person at least five thousand dollars. How did this bizarre situation come about?

It seems to have been the end product of an extremely shrewd woman's passion for expensive clothing, combined with yearning for publicity on the part of designers. Long before the Reagan era, admirers and people wanting favors began showering gifts on the residents of the White House. Andrew Jackson, whose beloved wife died before his inauguration, once received a cheese that weighed more than one thousand pounds. Old Hickory soon held an open house that drew a mob of guests, who gobbled down every bit of the cheese. Later, Abraham Lincoln was the surprised recipient of a jackass sent to him by a minor potentate. He named the animal Royal Gift and turned him over to Union soldiers who hitched him to a supply wagon.

After public protests against gifts to elected officials began to mount, Congress passed the Ethics in Government Act. Officials of the federal government are now required to include any gift valued at thirty-five dollars or more on an annual disclosure statement made in April. The lawmakers worded the law so that intangible gratuities such as expense-paid trips given to them are not covered. The language concerning gifts made to the spouse of the chief executive is ambiguous, perhaps through oversight, perhaps by design.

In 1981 as the first year of their tenure in the White House drew to a close, attorneys advised Ronald and Nancy Reagan of the law concerning tangible gifts. They are also believed to have warned them that such gifts might have to be reported to the Internal Revenue Service as income.

In February 1982, the first lady announced that she would accept no more gifts from designers, jewelers, and other "personal benefactors." She said that she would accept loans of such things as designer originals but would return them after use.

The reporters for *Time* magazine dug through the disclosure forms and tax records for 1982 through 1987. Their summary said that they could find no evidence that any of the first lady's clothing and jewelry had been listed as gifts or as loans.

The White House response was issued by Ellen Crispen, press secretary to Nancy Reagan. The first lady had assured her, said Crispen, that she had not received valuable gifts or loans since being informed about the regulations concerning them.

Perhaps because no chief executive since FDR has been so venerated as Ronald Reagan, the public reaction to the revelations in *Time* was muted. Mamie Eisenhower's nonexistent "chronic alcoholism" was given much more space nationally than was Nancy Reagan's flouting of the law.

Many admirers fondly remembered that in 1968—long before she entered the White House—Nancy was listed among the best dressed women of America. Even her detractors admired her youthful figure, the one-of-a-kind tint she used on her hair, and her capacity to look absolutely dazzling when dressed in red. With billions having replaced millions when the federal budget was being discussed, many people believed it was ridiculous to make noise about a few dresses. Those who provided the outfits were of the same view, but they conceded that many more than a "few" items were involved.

Former Adolfo executive Oscar de Lavin estimated that from that designer alone, she received as much as one hundred thousand dollars worth of originals annually. The value of the Galanos satin inaugural ballgown was estimated as at least twenty-five thousand dollars. Although no appraisal of it was ever made public, an emerald necklace given to the first lady by Imelda Marcos of the Philippines is believed to have been worth more than fifty thousand dollars.

There is documentary evidence that Nancy actually treated a few things as loans, which were returned to their owners after use. A white mink jacket was sent back to Galanos after having been worn once. Diamond jewelry worth nearly five hundred thousand

Nancy Reagan, ready to vote for her husband in his first try for elective office in California. [ASSOCIATED PRESS]

dollars that Nancy displayed at her husband's first inaugural ball was returned to Harry Winston.

After her pledge to accept only loans in lieu of gifts, the first lady from California sent more than a dozen outfits to New York. There Anne Keagy, earlier head of the Parsons School of Design, had agreed to send borrowed finery to museums on a rotating basis. The satin gown worn in 1981 went to the Smithsonian Institution's permanent display of first ladies' inaugural gowns.

Designer David Hayes of Los Angeles pointed out that after an original has made a single appearance, its sale value drops to nothing. For practical purposes, this means that designers have no reason to want their originals returned after they have been worn. Other fashion designers assured reporters that although they received no monies from the first lady, they were extremely well paid. Payment came in the form of publicity they could not have financed for twice the price of the gifts and "loans."

The first lady, of course, was aware of these economic factors. She made additional token payments to makers of exclusive finery by seeing that they received invitations to exclusive White House entertainments.

One fashion industry analyst considered the matter of Mrs. Reagan's originals to be a huge joke. "Cervantes inserted an appropriate line in *Don Quixote*," he suggested. "Somewhere in that marvelous story, the author has one of his characters say to another: 'When they offer thee a heifer, run with a halter [in order to lead your gift home quickly].'"

Offered a whole herd of heifers by designers, Nancy Reagan seems to have kept a supply of halters on her arm, ready for use at all times. Without alluding to any laws concerning tangible gifts, she often pointed out that European royalty and heads of state take valuable gifts for granted. There was no reason why she should act differently, she said. If the journalistic exposure in 1988 had an effect on the tax status of the president and the first lady, it was not made public.

Americans seem not to be cut from the same cloth as their forefathers. In 1840 Congressman Charles Ogle of Pennsylvania made a speech about "The Royal Splendors of the President's Palace." His oratorical fires had been lighted by Martin Van Buren's request for money from Congress to make essential improvements to the Executive Mansion and its grounds.

Van Buren's urge to spend $3,665 may have contributed to his defeat in his bid for reelection. Nancy Reagan's acceptance of questionable gifts and loans worth three hundred times as much was shrugged aside by twentieth-century voters.

29

Dolley to Eleanor

Endorsements and Legacies

*O*ver the years clever businessmen have discovered that attaching the name of a first lady to their produce could increase sales. The first such venture involved Dolley Madison and the new culinary delight, ice cream. A snuff manufacturer soon followed suit.

There's no evidence that the widow of James Madison knew that her name was being exploited. Her temperament was such, however, that the dowager queen of capital society probably would not have bristled at being offered Dolley Madison Ice Cream or Dolley Madison Snuff. Chances are that she would have flashed a winsome smile and observed, "With a name like that, it *has* to be good!"

Martha Washington had no opportunity to test the quality of flour bearing her name. Manufacture of that product did not start until years after her death, possibly triggered by the success of Dolley Madison snuff.

Four years before she married the widowed president John Tyler, Julia Gardiner was featured in an 1840 advertisement. A handbill, manually tinted, depicted her on the arm of a swain walking in front of the Boget and Mecamly Department Store in Manhattan. She carried on her left forearm a frilled placard announcing, "I'll purchase at Boget & Mecamly's, No. 86 9th Avenue. Their goods are Beautiful and Astonishingly Cheap."

Dolley Madison's name was used to help sell ice cream.
[JAMES PEALE PORTRAIT]

Later, as first lady, she said the advertising print was produced without her knowledge or permission. Considerable evidence suggests, however, that she willingly posed for the store's artist. Such a step would have been consistent with the temperament of the first lady who began the custom of having the Marine Corps band play "Hail to the Chief" whenever the president appeared on a ceremonial occasion.

Shortly after the Civil War a special device facilitating household ironing was devised. Metal more than an inch thick and shaped like a boat with a flat bottom was equipped with a removable wooden handle. This meant that while ironing was being done, another implement could be heated on the stove. When the first iron cooled, a change of handles meant a hot iron could go to work while its companion was being reheated. It came to be called a "sad iron" from a German word meaning "heavy."

By the time Lucy and Rutherford Hayes were in residence at the White House, it was in demand throughout the North. In an early and unauthorized "celebrity endorsement," the first family was depicted discussing the purchase of a sad iron while on a visit to Philadelphia.

A New York department store advertisement featured the future Mrs. John Tyler as one of its satisfied customers.

A brouhaha resulted from the unauthorized use of Frances Folsom Cleveland's name in advertising. Her June 2, 1886, White House marriage ceremony created interest throughout the nation. Inevitably, her portrait soon appeared in an advertisement that suggested the new mistress of the White House, known affectionately as Frankie, was a user of Sulphur Bitters.

Advertisers could not wait to jump on the Frankie bandwagon by using her name to persuade buyers to choose their candy, soap, ladies' underwear, perfume, and numerous other products. Frances and Grover Cleveland tolerated her exploitation until a maker of arsenic pills claimed that they were responsible for her beautiful complexion.

Furious, in 1888 the president persuaded his allies in Congress to introduce special legislation that stipulated: "Any individual or

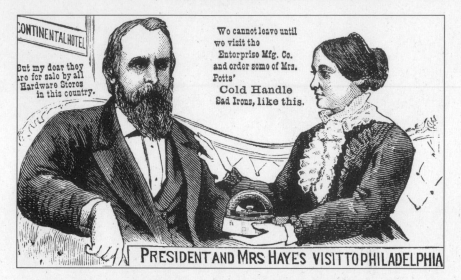

Manufacturers depicted Rutherford and Lucy Hayes touting their sad iron.

corporation who shall publicly exhibit, use or employ the likeness or representation of any female—living or dead—who is or was the wife, mother, daughter, or sister of any citizen of the U.S. without the consent in writing of the person so depicted shall be guilty of high misdemeanor." Upon indictment, an advertiser was to pay a fine of five hundred dollars to five thousand dollars "and stand imprisoned until fine and costs are paid."

Before this piece of "Frances Cleveland legislation" came to a vote, however, constitutional scholars condemned it. As the wife of a president, they pointed out, she fell into the unprotected category of a public figure. This argument proved so convincing that the measure designed to shield Cleveland's bride was never enacted.

Manufacturers seized upon the rebuff as an invitation to indulge themselves. With patent medicines and soaps leading the pack, a wide variety of products were advertised in ways that suggested they were the favorites of the first lady. Cleveland fumed that he would sue everyone who took advantage of his bride in this fashion. Soon persuaded that he would be wasting time and money, the president tried to avoid seeing new ads that included the portrait or name of Frankie.

After Cleveland won a nonconsecutive second term in 1892, his wife was subjected to a final indignity that may have annoyed her

Eleanor Roosevelt boosted public confidence in air travel in general and American Airways in particular. [FRANKLIN D. ROOSEVELT LIBRARY]

more than all the earlier ones. Her small daughter Ruth became a focus of public attention so great that it was risky to have her seen in public.

One day a nursemaid was with the tot on the south lawn of the White House when a party of tourists approached. Watching from an upstairs window, the horrified first lady saw a woman attempt to seize her baby—probably but not positively wanting nothing more than a close look. Headlines about Baby Ruth Cleveland inspired a candy manufacturer to give the name of Frances Cleveland's daughter to their product, still a popular confection.

Eleanor Roosevelt had to know that she was boosting the prestige of American Airways when she took a flight to Dallas soon after becoming first lady and willingly posed beside the plane that took her there. Since she was one of a tiny handful of female frequent fliers in that period, the photo boosting the prestige of American Airways attracted attention and possibly passengers everywhere it appeared.

Part 5

First Ladies Betrayed

Warren G. Harding was not an ambitious politician and his administration was swamped with scandal, including some longtime affairs.

30

Flossie Harding

Carrie and Nan

*J*im Phillips, son of a blacksmith, was determined to make something of himself. Reared twenty-five miles west of Marion, Ohio, he moved to Huntington, Indiana, and found a job in a dry goods store. He saved every penny possible, and in 1885 came to Marion to set up a business of his own in partnership with a friend. It took only a few years for Uhler, Phillips, and Company to become the largest dry-goods business in the town of fifteen thousand.

Jim waited until 1896 to marry Carrie Fulton of Bucyrus, nine years his junior. Carrie brought home nearly twenty dollars a month from teaching school and was very attractive by almost everyone's standards.

Warren G. Harding, publisher of the *Marion Star* congratulated Phillips on "making a whale of a success in business and marriage." Although they were almost exactly the same age, Phillips looked up to his Republican friend because Harding had been courageous enough to run for the office of county auditor in a heavily Democratic county.

In 1892 Harding had married divorcée Florence Mabel Kling DeWolf, who was five years his senior and had a ten-year-old son. Flossie, as her husband and friends called her, glowed with pride when her husband won a seat in the Ohio state senate in 1899. "From the first time I saw him I was sure he would make a name in politics," she told her nearly grown son. Warren's new status

Florence "Flossie" Harding was intimately acquainted with her husband's first lover.

encouraged her to buy the finest clothes and give the fanciest parties of anyone in Marion.

Although her health was never the best, she developed serious kidney trouble in 1905, during Harding's term as lieutenant governor. Hoping to free his mind of problems at home, at the capital, and at the *Star,* he often told his black driver to "crank up the old car" and to drive him to Bucyrus.

Because Bucyrus was Carrie Phillips's birthplace, her husband had purchased a nice home there. While he still did business in Huntington, he would try to spend time there with her whenever he could get away. His enterprise, however, was doing so well that he and his partner were beginning to talk of possibly opening a branch in New York City. Phillips then suffered a bad attack of nerves and decided to get treatment at Battle Creek, Michigan.

While their spouses were being restored to health, Harding and Carrie discovered that they were attracted to each other. For the next fifteen years they met discreetly at every opportunity. It appeared that Flossie and Phillips did not suspect the affair.

In 1907 the Hardings went abroad. When they returned, Flossie, or Duchess, as Harding called her, raved about the voyage. Carrie

Phillips convinced her husband that a similar voyage would be good for his nerves. Thus, in February 1909 the Hardings and the Phillipses sailed from New York together. After a Mediterranean tour they passed through Italy and Switzerland and into Germany. "This is where I belong!" Carrie announced.

After the two couples returned to Ohio, Harding began writing poems dedicated to Carrie. When they found it difficult to meet, he wrote letters to "Sis," signing them with his initials. These letters did not surface again until 1963. Harding was comfortable with the arrangement until Carrie began to press him to divorce Flossie. When that failed to happen, she left her husband and moved to Berlin.

In 1914 Harding was elected to the U.S. Senate and believed this to be the summit of his political ambition. He was also heartbroken by Carrie's absence; however, he found consolation when a schoolgirl enthusiastically revealed her own infatuation with him. Nan Britton, thirty years his junior and twenty years younger than Carrie, was a strikingly beautiful blonde. When she finished her studies at a New York secretarial school, Senator Harding saw to it that she found a nice job and was rewarded with a delightful evening in a Manhattan hotel. Nan subsequently claimed that two years later, during one of her visits to the senator in his Washington office, she became pregnant. Years later it was discovered that Harding regularly sent child support money to Nan.

In the meantime, Carrie Phillips had returned to Ohio shortly before the outbreak of World War I. By then Harding was a U.S. senator. With the issue of war being debated in Congress, she threatened to reveal their longtime affair if Harding voted to declare war on Germany. Harding voted for war, and Carrie backed down, but they revived their affair until 1920 when he received his party's nomination for the presidency.

Duchess had been instrumental in convincing him that he should run, but both Harding and the Republican leadership knew that his candidacy could be damaged by the revelation of the affair with Carrie Phillips. A meeting was arranged, and some high-ranking officials of the party reputedly gave the Phillipses twenty thousand dollars, promised additional monthly payments, and sent the reunited couple on a leisurely trip to Japan.

Once Flossie and the former senator were established in the White House, Harding may have continued his liaisons with Nan with the assistance of Secret Service agents.

Warren G. Harding was hailed by the press as "the epitome of middle-class American dignity."

When her distinguished lover died under somewhat peculiar circumstances on August 2, 1923, Nan Britton demanded fifty thousand dollars from his estate, not for herself, she told the relatives of the late chief executive, but as a trust fund for the child she had borne. The two parties failed to reach an agreement. Angered, Nan wrote a two-hundred-thousand-word account of her affair with Harding. The epic was circulated among several publishing houses, but none would publish it.

Nan refused to abandon her project and finally found a backer who put up ten thousand dollars to defray production expenses. In 1927 *The President's Daughter* was ready for the bookstores. Book buyers, however, were as cautious as publishers and hesitant to stock the book until the *Baltimore Sun* ran a long article about it by H. G. Mencken. It then sold an estimated eighty-five thousand copies.

Whether or not Nan Britton's account was accurate, there is little doubt that Harding was engaged in a long and torrid affair with her and Carrie Phillips. Flossie may not have known about the affairs. On the other hand, there is a possibility that she was aware of her husband's infidelities. Rumors abounded that Harding's death was the result of his wife's malice. What the Duchess herself described as the "convulsive twitching of his mouth" before his death in San Francisco, her later refusal to permit an autopsy of his body, and the wholesale destruction of many of his confidential records fueled the suspicion that she might have poisoned her husband.

Florence Harding died sixteen months after her husband, on November 21, 1924, a victim of a persistent kidney disease. She and her husband were the second presidential couple to die prior to the completion of their first term in the White House.

31

Mamie Eisenhower

The Rival Jeep Driver

*T*he relatives crowded into a Denver home said that they felt like "cheering at a football game." Nineteen-year-old Mamie Doud, they proudly assured one another, said her wedding vows "like no other bride ever said them." When she kissed her husband, she whispered only three words into his ear: "Forever and ever!"

Dwight D. Eisenhower, age twenty-six and a second lieutenant in the U.S. Army, glowed almost as much as his bride, but he was less demonstrative. After Mamie's tearful parting with her parents, John and Elvira Doud, the happy couple drove to Abilene, Kansas, and met Ike's family. Soon Mamie found herself mistress of a two-room apartment in the married officers barracks at Fort Sam Houston, Texas.

Nineteen homes and twenty-seven years later, in 1943 she received from her husband a letter that she read and reread with tearful disbelief. Writing from London after nearly a year of absence from the woman he still fondly called "my fast-stepping little bride," he went to considerable length to deny gossip.

With the world in confusion, he pointed out, it was easy for rumors to get started and all but impossible to put an end to them. His "poor brain," he wrote, was too full of important matters to make room for ridiculous tales. When Allied forces were victorious, promised General Eisenhower, he would hurry home and give Mamie a detailed account of everything he had done.

At age eighteen Mamie Doud was widely admired as "the belle of San Antonio."

Mamie desperately wanted to believe Ike, but could not. Too many stories, differing in details but similar in emphasis, were floating across the Atlantic and reaching Washington. Most of them claimed that Eisenhower was having an affair with his chauffeur; a few insisted that he was in love with her and would seek a divorce.

Mamie's face took on a bit of her girlhood glow every time she opened one of many letters written to "the Girl I love more today than when I married you in 1916." Yet these assurances never fully dispelled her doubts. Too many sources were saying too many things to let her regain her earlier peace of mind.

Trouble started almost as soon as Lieutenant General Eisenhower went overseas to North Africa and had a group of drivers assigned to him. Since able-bodied men were needed to fight, his drivers were women. Both Inez Scott and Pearlie Hagrave were members of the fast-growing service called WACS. A petite blonde of twenty-five, Pearlie was engaged and later married. English-born Elsbeth Duncan was a capable driver but described as "too stiff and formal, not yet at ease in military life."

An unknown photographer snapped a fuzzy image of Eisenhower and Summersby in North Africa.

Kay Summersby, a native of Ireland's County Cork, was a divorcée but engaged. She mastered the handling of Ike's jeep in less than two hours. Everyone who saw Kay was impressed by her slender figure. One longtime acquaintance insisted that her high cheekbones, "similar to those of Garbo," made her appear incongruous in uniform. With a mass of dark red hair, when Kay occasionally donned semiformal dress for evening functions, "she looked like anything but a jeep driver."

When her fiancé was killed in 1943, Eisenhower did his best to comfort his grieving driver. The secretarial duties assigned to her, he later explained, were designed to help get her mind off her personal tragedy. Her new duties also meant that she spent more time with the general. By the time Ike and his driver-secretary left North Africa for England, gossip began circulating about them.

Living the lonely life of an "army widow" for more than three years, Mamie probably would have paid no attention to a single innuendo, but when Ike-and-Kay jokes began appearing in *Stars and Stripes* and other media, she became perturbed. In response to one of her letters, her husband wrote: "Darling, stop worrying about me. The few women I've met are nothing—absolutely nothing—

compared to you. Besides, I've neither the time nor the youth to worry about them. I love you—always."

By the time Mamie became mistress of the White House in 1953, Kay Summersby was old news. In 1948 Kay published her story under the title *Eisenhower Was My Boss,* which supported none of the stories of Eisenhower's infidelity. Eisenhower died in 1969. A few years later, Kay Summersby hired a ghostwriter and revised and rewrote her memoirs. This new edition was entitled *Past Forgetting—My Love Affair with Dwight D. Eisenhower.* She described their romance in detail.

Kay's death in 1974 delayed publication until 1976. It then attracted sufficient attention to serve as the basis for a television miniseries in 1979.

Mamie, age seventy-seven when the tell-all Summersby book appeared, endured it with more tranquility than her friends expected. Since the revised volume lacked documentation, only two persons—Ike and Kay—ever knew the truth about their relationship. She told friends, "I treasure memories of my own that no other woman shares with me. When Ike and I celebrated our golden wedding anniversary in 1966, I'm positive that his jeep driver never once entered his mind."

32

Eleanor Roosevelt

Lucy, You Got Some 'Splaining to Do

*E*leanor Roosevelt was ill at ease when she and her husband arrived in Washington in 1913. She knew little about protocol in the capital, and she was keenly aware of her ignorance. Her husband was Woodrow Wilson's new assistant secretary of the navy, and they would immediately become a part of both the political and the social whirl.

She was expected to attend dinners and receptions, christenings of ships, and many other functions. Eleanor was painfully shy and self-conscious, her clothes were unfashionable, and her face was anything but beautiful. To compound her difficulties, she wore a brace to compensate for what may have been scoliosis, a defect of the spine and shoulders. Always high-pitched, her voice rose to a shrill squeak when she was agitated.

To overcome some of her personal liabilities, Eleanor threw herself into volunteer activities. During the Great War she spent many hours at canteens for soldiers, knitted for the Red Cross, and became a supporter of the suffrage movement.

Her increasingly heavy schedule led her to seek the help of a social secretary. She chose a widow of twenty-two. Lucy Page Mercer had an impeccable background, with family connections in the capital's aristocracy. Lucy was also very attractive. Her voice was described as "a lot like dark velvet," and she had the warm charm that folklore attributes to women of the South.

Regardless of her emotions, Eleanor Roosevelt usually managed to look serene.

Initially working for Eleanor three mornings a week, Lucy soon proved herself an efficient assistant and also became a friend, not only of the five Roosevelt children, but their parents as well. She was often included in Eleanor's luncheons and dinner parties. This cordial relationship continued until Lucy resigned to become a yeoman third class and do her bit for the war effort.

In July 1918 Franklin Roosevelt made an inspection tour of naval operations overseas. When he returned home in September, utterly exhausted, he had a high fever. Diagnosed as double pneumonia, he was hospitalized. When Eleanor unpacked his bags, she discovered a packet of letters written to Franklin by Lucy.

Initially devastated, upon reflection Eleanor blamed herself for what she considered an illicit love affair. When Franklin began to regain his strength, she told him that she had read and destroyed the correspondence and offered to give him an uncontested divorce.

Franklin realized that a divorce would likely bring his political career to a halt. He also knew that Lucy was Catholic, opposed to divorce, and there was no reason to believe she would be a party to scandal. Another woman also had to be taken into consideration. Sara Delano Roosevelt, Franklin's strong-willed mother, was

Franklin D. Roosevelt was the first chief executive to be lauded as a great communicator.
[NATIONAL ARCHIVES]

in firm control of the family fortune. When rumors of the difficulty between her son and his wife reached her, she announced that if he and Eleanor were divorced, he would not inherit a nickel.

Eventually Eleanor and Franklin reached an agreement. Their marriage would remain intact on condition that he sever all ties with Lucy Mercer.

Elected governor of New York in 1929, Eleanor's husband was a natural choice as the Democratic nominee for the presidency in 1932. On November 8 Herbert Hoover lost by such a landslide that Roosevelt knew he had a mandate for radical change.

Reelected three more times, Eleanor's husband created the New Deal, and in doing so he carved his initials on nearly every aspect of American life. To him, some of his social legislation was almost as significant as the Allied victory in World War II.

Soon after becoming first lady, Eleanor launched a series of tours that became so extensive she was derided as "Rover" by J. Edgar Hoover. No other wife of a president had flown in an airplane, but she logged more than half a million miles in them. By traveling throughout the country she became the eyes and ears of her polio-confined husband, keeping him in touch with the thinking of the American people. Beginning in 1935, she wrote a syndicated newspaper column, "My Day," in which she often alluded to

Roosevelt in the swimming pool at Warm Springs, Georgia.

her radio addresses. Her frequent speeches to large audiences brought her fees of one thousand dollars per appearance.

Long before they entered the White House, Eleanor and Franklin began having separate vacations. She liked to spend a few days at Campobello; he preferred to visit Bernard Baruch's plantation in South Carolina. There the president heard of the waters at nearby Warm Springs, Georgia, and how it seemed to help some polio victims.

With the help of George Foster Peabody and Henry Ford's son, Edsel, Roosevelt helped establish a combined resort and center for the treatment of polio. He built a modest white-frame cottage there and retreated to it at every opportunity.

Separated far more than they were together, Eleanor received a steady stream of notes addressed simply "Dear Babs." This term of endearment was his term for "Baby." From time to time a message included a casual reference to Lucy Mercer. Such comments seemed to Franklin to serve as a smokescreen; he was again seeing Lucy regularly. She was seen at the Baruch plantation and Warm Springs.

A wartime blackout of news concerning the activities of the U.S. commander in chief made it possible for Franklin and Lucy to meet more frequently. She even appeared in the White House as a dinner guest a number of times when Eleanor was away and her unsuspecting daughter was serving as hostess. Franklin may have introduced her to Winston Churchill during one of the many visits made by the British leader. According to columnist Joseph Alsop, the president divulged top-secret military information to the woman he adored but could never marry.

On April 12, 1945, President Roosevelt was sitting for a portrait at his beloved Warm Springs cottage, with Lucy by his side, when he suffered a fatal cerebral hemorrhage. By the time Eleanor arrived, Lucy had been spirited away by Secret Service agents.

33

Lady Bird

Alice and Company

Lady Bird, I want you to meet this long, tall drink of muddy water," Eugene Lassiter said.

Black-haired Claudia Alta Taylor, whose legal name hardly any of her friends knew, extended her hand. Towering five inches over her, her new acquaintance gave a big smile and drawled, "I'm Lyndon Johnson."

He squeezed Lady Bird's hand, bent to her level and whispered: "I'm taken tonight, but how about breakfast tomorrow at the Driskill?"

Regarded as being "decidedly on the plain side," partly because she almost always wore drab clothes, Lady Bird said nothing. At the University of Texas in Austin, where she had recently earned a degree in journalism, she had few male friends. This big fellow, an aide to Congressman Dick Kleburg, was acting as though she had swept him off his feet.

Although she had not promised to do so, Lady Bird showed up at the Hotel Driskill the following morning. During their leisurely breakfast they agreed to meet again at 2:30 P.M. Before the afternoon was over, Lyndon proposed marriage and Lady Bird did not say no.

Less than sixty days after they met at the home of a mutual friend, the two Texans became husband and wife in a San Antonio ceremony. Lyndon, who had forgotten to bring a ring, sent a friend to find one and then slipped on the bride's finger a wedding band that cost $2.98 at Sears, Roebuck and Company.

Lyndon B. Johnson was one of the most politically ambitious men of mid-twentieth-century America.

In Washington they found a one-bedroom apartment they could afford and set up housekeeping. Soon Lady Bird was involved in the political activities of her ambitious husband. She attended parties and receptions, but she especially enjoyed showing visiting Texans the sights of the capital.

Lyndon had congressional ambitions but no money to stage a campaign. When Lady Bird received an inheritance, she put up ten thousand dollars and he won a 1937 contest. He had occupied a seat in the House of Representatives only a short time before wealthy Charles E. Marsh requested the freshman lawmaker to visit his office in the Mayfair Hotel. Lyndon responded immediately, knowing that the *Austin American-Statesman,* the most influential newspaper in his congressional district, was among the many Marsh holdings.

Old enough to be Lyndon's father, Marsh was a self-made millionaire who owned a country estate, Longlea, in the Virginia hunt country. He invited the congressman and his wife to visit there.

Six years earlier Marsh had fallen in love with Alice Glass, a beautiful woman who was almost six feet tall. He divorced his wife, took Alice as his lover, and let her design and name his country manor house. It was breathtaking in a quietly elegant way. Its walls

Alice Glass was simultaneously the mistress of a wealthy publisher and LBJ.

were hung with paintings by Old Masters and its stables were filled with spirited horses. A huge swimming pool was a favorite haunt of the mistress of the mansion, who dressed formally for dinner and draped herself with jewels. Despite repeated entreaties, Alice refused to marry Marsh but bore him two children.

Soon Lady Bird was surprised but took no offense when Lyndon accepted a weekend invitation at Longlea when she was scheduled to conduct a tour of Jefferson's Monticello for constituents from Texas. That weekend proved to be the first of many. Any time Marsh was away for an extended business trip, Alice sent for Lyndon. Often but not always, prominent visitors were also guests.

Charles Marsh seems to have had no idea that the awkward and gangling politician and his stately young mistress were having an affair. Lady Bird may have suspected infidelity but did not wish to issue a challenge.

At Longlea, Alice often read the poetry of Edna St. Vincent Millay to her new lover, only three years her senior. She gave him advice concerning his clothing and slowly guided him toward improving his table manners.

Their intimate relationship continued until Alice realized his political career was foremost in Lyndon's life. She agreed to marry Marsh. During the dozen years Johnson spent in the U.S. Senate they maintained their relationship. Initially delighted when her lover won the presidency in 1964, Alice seems to have lost her ardor for him when he stepped up the pace of U.S. involvement in Vietnam. Some observers suggested the president no longer needed Marsh as his backer or Alice as his lover. He was at the pinnacle of his career and there were several interesting women around him.

Regardless of how many other conquests he made, except for Lady Bird, Johnson seems to have had only one real love. That he may have parted with Alice because of differences over national policy is one of the many inconsequential unknowns that shroud the Johnson presidency.

34

Jacqueline Kennedy

Grace and Rejection

*J*acqueline Lee Bouvier's educational record included study at elite institutions. After five years in private academies, she went to Vassar and then to the Sorbonne in Paris. When she made her debut at New York's Clambake Club, society columnist "Cholly Nickerbocker" named her "the Queen Deb of 1947." Then although she did not have to work, she took a job at the *Washington Times-Herald* as an inquiring camera girl.

At a dinner in the home of journalist Charles Bartlett, she met John F. Kennedy, a war hero who had been elected to the U.S. House in 1946. After a sporadic courtship during which he was elected to the Senate, they were married in a fashionable wedding in September 1953.

Seven years later, he won the White House, and three years later he was felled by an assassin's bullet. Silence had blanketed the extramarital activities of the dashing young president, but once he was gone, stories began to surface.

The first to make public her relationship was Judith Campbell (later Exner), who announced that she paid the first of two dozen surreptitious visits to the White House four months after Kennedy had entered the mansion. She may have gone public with her story after a Senate select committee began to look into the activities of Momo "Sam" Giancana, because she was also Giancana's mistress. Since the Federal Bureau of Investigation was exploring possible organized crime connections with the Kennedy assassination,

John F. Kennedy was described as "able to win almost any woman he wanted with one glance."

Campbell was investigated as well. In 1967 her book, *My Story*, was published. Although much of the account cannot be corroborated, some people agree that it includes details that could have been learned only in Kennedy's bedroom.

Mary Pinchot Meyer, a lovely divorced Washington socialite, lived next door to Robert Kennedy, the president's brother and attorney general, who is believed to have smuggled her into the White House for the first time in January 1962. Meyer, whose former husband was an aide to Harold E. Stassen, was later quoted as saying that she was attracted to the president by his "unwavering attention" when face to face with her. If her story is credible, during a period of nearly eighteen months, she entered the mansion through a door at the southwest corner every two to three weeks.

There was nothing surreptitious about the Madison Square Garden celebration of Kennedy's forty-fifth birthday in 1962. The biggest Democratic fundraiser of the period and held on May 19 (ten days early), the bash brought in more than one million dollars.

Hundreds of political celebrities and entertainment stars joined in festivities that were topped by the appearance of Marilyn Monroe.

Although described as being tipsy, Monroe managed to use the melody of "Thanks for the Memory" to stumble through a song that thanked the president for winning battles of the cold war, defeating U.S. Steel in the courts, and solving "our problems by the ton."

Later that year the thirty-six-year-old actress allegedly committed suicide. One of her former husbands, Joe DiMaggio, angrily demanded that all members of the Kennedy family stay away from her funeral. Investigators later found telephone records of her many calls to the White House and acquaintances began leaking accounts of her clandestine meetings with the president.

Both *Time* and *Newsweek* published exposés concerning Kennedy's marital infidelities. The president was alleged to have found many women eager to go to bed with him. Secretaries Priscilla Wear and Jill Cowan (said to have used the code names Fiddle and Faddle for their trysts) were among White House staffers named, as was Jacqueline's press secretary. The list also included an airline stewardess, stripper Blaze Starr, and socialite Florence Pritchett.

Five years after Kennedy's assassination, Jackie married Greek shipping billionaire Aristotle Onassis. Members of the general public, not yet aware of what the dead president's wife had tolerated, searched for words to express their indignation and scorn. Many Americans who cherish memories of the fabled "Camelot years" still feel a sense of betrayal because the lovely young widow who fashioned that image appeared to reject it.

Part 6

First Ladies and the White House

The President's House in 1841 was never really home to William Henry Harrison, who gave way to John and Letitia Tyler. [LIBRARY OF CONGRESS]

35

Abigail to Jacqueline

Fun and Food

White House entertainment runs the gamut from simple and inexpensive to elaborate and costly. Formal dinners, receptions, informal dinners, musicales, and other events have traditionally been arranged under the supervision of the mistress of the mansion. Guests typically arrive expecting both fun and food. In the beginning, there was little fun and not a trace of food.

Members of French royalty were long formally greeted upon arising from bed. From a term meaning "to rise," such ceremonies came to be called a levee. English monarchs picked up the term and applied it to formal receptions, usually staged at court.

The British influence in North America remained strong for many years after the American Revolution. As a result, Martha Washington's first receptions, held in New York, were known as levees. She usually stayed in the background after arranging for the president to stand before a fireplace.

Attendance was by invitation or letter of introduction; guests seldom exceeded a score in number. In New York, they arrived on Tuesdays at 2 P.M.; when the capital was moved to Philadelphia, the time set for welcoming guests became 3 P.M. Once inside the president's house, they stood in a circle.

Precisely fifteen minutes after the front door was opened for the first arrival, it was locked. Guests then advanced one by one toward the president. Each solemnly bowed, then backed into place. When all had paid homage, the president walked among his

211

Martha Washington, right, kept both hands full to avoid shaking hands with guests.

guests, often bowing but not speaking except to call their names. To prevent anyone from trying to shake hands with him, during a levee Washington rested one hand on the hilt of his dress sword, the other on his hat.

Abigail Adams continued to hold levees, usually weekly, in a curved Philadelphia room built for the purpose. She also initiated the custom of having a less formal reception on January 1. Abigail's punch bowls were the first source of festivity, and proved so popular that the New Year's Day reception was traditional for more than a century.

Discontinued under the regime of widower Thomas Jefferson, the levee was revived by Julia Tyler, but she held it only once a month instead of weekly. To the consternation of Washington society, Julia "upset all the forms" by standing with her attendants in a line across the Blue Room. This expedient shifted her husband from the exposed center of the room and put him at the head of a receiving line.

Mary Todd Lincoln honored tradition by regularly holding levees, but she made it a practice to stand far to one side so she would not have to shake hands with her guests. Eliza Johnson decided that her levees would be open to all comers, making these stiffly formal affairs more relaxed, but these were the last "entertainments" of this sort. Julia Grant dropped the custom of holding levees at regular intervals, and no successor revived it.

Elizabeth Monroe was first to plan an entertainment for visiting Native Americans. Sixteen men came to Washington City from the West as tribal representatives. An Oto chieftain brought along his young wife and watched in amazement as Eagle of Delight charmed the gathering at the New Year's Reception of 1821.

Rachel Jackson had been buried at the Hermitage near Nashville on Christmas Eve 1828, shortly before Andrew Jackson left for his inauguration. He announced that he wanted nothing to do with entertainments in the mansion. Slaves brought from Tennessee replaced the staff of experienced household servants. Although they knew nothing about protocol, Jackson's servants were skilled cooks, and they prepared the first truly memorable White House feast.

Mobs of eager admirers engulfed the President's House when Andrew Jackson took up residency.

Thousands of admirers had flocked to the capital to pay their respects to Jackson, the hero of the battle of New Orleans. Many of these visitors had never been to the nation's capital before. Not knowing what to expect, numbers of them brought along their own liquid refreshments.

When the doors were opened in the afternoon for the inaugural reception, a stream of humanity burst into the mansion. Elegantly dressed Washingtonians were shoved aside by the eager mob of rough frontiersmen.

Arrivals at a reception usually dwindled to a trickle after about an hour and a half; not so in 1829. Instead of diminishing, the crush increased. They stood on chairs, broke china, tore draperies, and even pushed the president aside. Jackson took refuge in the oval drawing room and was trapped by a wall of admirers who stood shoulder to shoulder.

The visitors soon emptied barrels of lemonade and orange punch, well laced with whiskey. Some who had never before seen ice cream accepted the delicacy gingerly, then smacked their lips loudly as they began to sample it. When every room was filled to capacity, late arrivals were forced to remain in the yard. So many were packed so closely together that every shrub and small tree was trampled.

On this occasion and at many later entertainments, there were no preparations for what might be called security. People simply pushed through a door and began roaming about the mansion. Even the living quarters were inspected by the curious.

The editors of the *Washington City Chronicle* described Jackson's reception, staged without any planning by a first lady, as a disaster. Socialite Margaret Bayard Smith fumed that "the noisy and disorderly rabble in the President's House brought to my mind descriptions of mobs in the Tuileries and at Versailles."

Twenty years later Julia Tyler, who considered her modification of the levee to represent a major triumph, decided to make her final ball the talk of the capital. With James Knox Polk slated to succeed her husband in office in March, the president's wife began planning the big event in January, six weeks in advance.

More than two thousand handwritten invitations were sent out for Julia's big bash, scheduled for February 18, 1845. So many high-ranking government officials, foreign diplomats, and military officers arrived with their wives on their arms that the mansion was crowded past capacity with three thousand guests.

Four rooms decorated for dancing and promenading were lighted with six hundred candles. John Tyler later grumbled that the candles alone cost him $350. He never recorded the cost of wine, which was available in open barrels. Neither did he say how much eight dozen bottles of champagne added to his bill for the evening.

After a nod to the conductor of the Marine Corps band, whose members wore scarlet uniforms, Julia accepted the arm of Secretary of War William Wilkins. Once the pair "opened the ball," the satin-clad first lady graciously danced a few steps with many gentlemen, even if she did not know their names.

Guests later said that the highlight of the most brilliant entertainment ever held in Washington came about midnight, when Julia and other ladies danced a cotillion with ambassadors from France, Russia, Prussia, and Austria.

Even Gen. Winfield Scott and Mirabeau B. Lamar, the former president of the Republic of Texas, applauded the gracefully whirling dancers. Francis P. Blair, editor of the *Washington Globe* and famous as a political kingmaker, termed Julia's ball "a fitting farewell for a beautiful first lady."

No one needed to tell Julia Grant that she was no latter-day Julia Tyler; she was self-conscious about her crossed eyes that Ulysses said he liked and did not want changed by surgery. Having decided to make her weekly receptions "truly republican in nature," Julia brought wives of cabinet members into receiving lines. No invitations were required; these affairs were open to anyone who cared to attend.

State dinners planned by Julia were a lot less than "truly republican," however. During her tenure as mistress of the mansion she entertained Queen Victoria's son, Prince Arthur, and Russia's Grand Duke Alexis, son of the czar. Another royal visitor, less significant on the world scene, was given an equally bountiful formal dinner. Returning to Hawaii, King Kalakaua spoke through an interpreter to say, "Mrs. Nellie certainly does know how to set a good table."

Alexis gave no interviews, but he must have shared the sentiments expressed by Kalakaua. In 1877 he came back to Washington with the Grand Duke Constantine in tow. At the formal dinner planned for them, the new first lady, Lucy Hayes, reluctantly yielded to entreaties by cabinet members and served wine instead of her customary lemonade.

Edith Roosevelt adopted Martha Washington's tactic of keeping her hands occupied at White House receptions.

Frances Cleveland approved of Julia Grant's "republican practices," and went a step further. Soon after she became mistress of the mansion, Frances began holding receptions for working women. The guests, who came without invitation, were on the job until Saturday noon. Hence the beautiful young first lady opened the mansion to them each Saturday afternoon and resisted pressure from officials who did not like to see the mansion "crowded with a great rabble of shop girls."

Soon after the turn of the century, Theodore Roosevelt's wife, Edith, gave receptions almost as large as Jackson's, but not as unruly. To keep her hands from aching after shaking so many hands, Edith held a bouquet with both hands.

Pablo Casals is remembered as having been the star guest at a musicale planned by Jacqueline Kennedy. Few who recall that event are aware that Casals earlier played at the White House by invitation of Edith Roosevelt. In addition to the cellist, Jacqueline brought to the mansion the Vienna Boys Choir, the Philadelphia Orchestra, and world-famous pianist Ignance Jan Paderewski.

Helen Taft was the first to combine a state dinner with a musicale, which followed the feast. In an era when antidiscriminatory practices were less strict, she refused to permit a bald waiter or butler to appear in the dining room of the mansion.

Lou Hoover found the traditional New Year's Day receptions "intolerable," so she abolished the custom. Her formal dinners, typically paid for by her husband, were a delight to the eye as well as the palate. Butlers and footmen, selected because each was exactly five feet eight inches tall, took off their black ties at dusk and donned white tails.

Convinced that any sounds made by servants would detract from the elegance of the occasion, Lou gave strict orders forbidding the clanging of silver. Before she left the mansion, she took her passion for silence to its ultimate. Instead of giving soft-spoken verbal directions to servants at the dinner table, she devised a system of hand signals to convey her orders to them.

A monarch inspired what many insiders remember as "the most elegant dinner ever held by a first lady." With President Mohammed Ayub Khan of Pakistan expected early in 1961, Jacqueline Kennedy decided to ignore precedent and stage it away from the White House.

A flotilla of three naval vessels and the presidential yacht took nearly 150 guests down the Potomac to Mount Vernon, home of George and Martha Washington. En route the guests sipped cocktails while listening to music by an orchestra. At the dinner, members of the party sat upon gilded ballroom chairs and feasted their eyes on tables decorated by Bonwit Teller and Tiffany's. This widely publicized event contributed substantially to Jacqueline's image as queen of a latter-day Camelot.

Betty Ford, propelled into the role of first lady in 1977 following the resignation of Richard Nixon, did not move into the White House until it was vacated by the former Julie Nixon and her husband, David Eisenhower. At her home in suburban Alexandria, Betty planned her first state dinner. Held in the White House by the woman not yet in residence there, it feted King Hussein of Jordan as the guest of honor.

36

Abigail to Barbara

Seldom Alone

Whether in the President's House or a private residence, few first ladies have been absolutely alone. Their beloved companions run the gamut of four-legged and two-legged creatures; understandably, dogs numerically head the list.

Abigail Adams gained both solace and companionship from her dog, Juno.

Lady Bird voiced no protest, but voters throughout the nation were horrified at Lyndon Johnson's treatment of two beagles. He casually picked Him and Her up by their ears in front of television cameras, unleashing a storm of protest from animal lovers across the country.

In one of his most famous speeches, Richard Nixon cited the family spaniel Checkers as the only gift of any consequence he had received during a campaign in which he was charged with accepting irregular contributions.

Grace Coolidge always smiled fondly when one of her white collies sauntered into a room. Rob Roy was named for a Scottish hero, but Prudence Prim got her name from her mincing walk. A chow was called Tiny Tim, and an Airedale answered to the name of Paul Pry.

Lyndon Johnson shows off the beagle Him to former president Dwight D. Eisenhower.

At her home in Buffalo, New York, Frances Cleveland kept a kennel full of pets. Frequently she brought at least four of them for White House visits: a Saint Bernard, a dachshund, a beagle, and a poodle. When friends came calling, Grover Cleveland's bride enjoyed demonstrating that her French poodle understood and obeyed commands in French.

Julia Tyler's favorite gift from her new husband was an Italian wolfhound, whom she affectionately called LaBeaux.

Lucy Hayes, who owned little jewelry, compensated for the lack of it by spending a great deal of time with her pooch, Gem.

Lou Hoover's dogs, Weegie and Pat, had the run of the mansion except during formal dinners or when ambassadors were in the receiving line of a reception.

Eleanor Roosevelt tolerated but never quite learned to love the two Irish setters that her husband insisted belonged to them jointly. When one of them bit the visiting Canadian prime minister,

Lou Hoover with her two dogs accompany the President in this candid White House photograph.

Eleanor turned her head and pretended that she had seen nothing. Fala, a Scottie, won the heart of the first lady—or so she said in her syndicated column, "My Day."

An English springer spaniel named Mildred Kerr, aka Millie, was considered first dog by Barbara Bush. That status was achieved when Millie delivered a litter during her White House days. She became famous when she "wrote" a book about Washington insiders, co-authored by her mistress. C. Fred Bush, a golden cocker spaniel named for C. Fred Chambers of Houston, was only the tip of a wet nose behind Millie in the first lady's affections.

In the roster of White House pets, birds follow dogs in number, but not closely. Dolley Madison's macaw, considered quite exotic in 1810, may have been the first bird frequently to perch on a first lady's shoulder.

Julia Tyler never revealed whether she loved her canary more than her wolfhound, but the doors of its cage were often opened so that Johnny Ty could fly from room to room in the President's House.

Frances Cleveland kept so many canaries and mockingbirds around the house that she lost count of their number despite knowing each of them by name.

Florence Harding, also a canary fancier, limited herself to two— Pete and Bob.

Grace Coolidge admitted that canaries named Nip, Tuck, and Snowflake were among her favorite companions, but she reserved a soft spot in her heart for Old Bill, a thrush.

Strangely, records include few references to cats as pampered pets of first ladies. That omission may be due to the fact that felines were working animals, brought into the mansion to reduce its sometimes large population of mice and rats. The exception was a big Siamese who belonged to Lucy Hayes; she would have sniffed disdainfully at the notion of pouncing upon a rodent.

Numerous hoofed pets have made their homes with first ladies. Grace Coolidge adored the red Shetland pony she long knew as Diana of Wildwood. After the animal stumbled several times, her mistress changed her name to Calamity Jane.

Julia Grant was fond of a spirited horse she called Psyche, but in her affections she leaned a trifle toward Missouri Belle.

A foreign potentate sent Mary Todd and Abraham Lincoln a jack- ass, whom they named Royal Gift but did not keep; they said the army needed it more than they did.

Edith Roosevelt never fully made up her mind whether or not she preferred her horse, Yagenka, to its stablemate called Nicollette.

Eleanor Roosevelt did not bring her mount named Dot to the White House. Instead she kept her at Fort Myers for convenience in cantering around Rock Creek Park.

Jacqueline Kennedy tethered the pony Macaroni on the White House lawn so the children could climb aboard at will. She herself liked to climb aboard Sadar, a gift from the king of Saudi Arabia.

Jacqueline Kennedy was an avid horsewoman and kept Sadar near the White House for frequent riding.
[JOHN F. KENNEDY LIBRARY]

Helen Taft permitted a Holstein cow to graze on the lawn.

Edith Wilson gave a herd of sheep the same privilege, explaining that she was helping the war effort by providing wool for soldiers' winter uniforms.

Edith Roosevelt smiled indulgently but did not scold when she learned that her fun-loving boys had used the White House elevator to smuggle a pony into an upstairs room.

The most bearded of all pets loved or tolerated by first ladies was a critter named Christopher Columbus. Lucy Hayes objected when someone said it did not seem proper to have a goat roaming about the lawn and gardens of the White House.

When she lived there, Caroline Harrison denied that a nameless goat that also had the run of the place belonged to her. "It's a favorite of my grandson," she told visitors.

Grace Coolidge with her raccoon, Rebecca.

A raccoon belonging to Grace Coolidge is among the most unusual of pets linked with first ladies. Still, top honors in this category probably go to Emily Spinach, a green snake that belonged to Edith Roosevelt.

37

Elizabeth to Nancy

The White House Dishes

At a break in the program of the 1982 Gridiron Dinner, an unannounced woman pranced from the wings and took center stage. One of the astonished reporters at the annual roast snapped a photo before jotting down a description:

> The apparition—for that is what it seemed to be—flounced about in an aqua skirt bearing huge flowers as its pattern. If anyone doubted that it was a she instead of an it, the white feather boa offered convincing evidence.
>
> A crimson headpiece bedecked with pinkish feathers and completed with a neat black bow seemed to shout: "Look at me . . . and listen!" Obviously having made her entrance in order to give a performance of some sort, the dazzling-drab little creature fingered a huge double strand of beads made brightly visible by a blood-red blouse. Someone in the audience rose and yelled: "It's Nancy!"

Ronald Reagan, who initially seems to have failed to recognize the first lady in her incredible rig, practically fell out of his chair with laughter. Earlier he seemed a bit grim as he heard his wife ridiculed about her wardrobe in a song that was a parody of "Second-Hand Rose."

When the guffaws began to subside, the performer, who obviously expected to take part in the program, affected a high falsetto voice and sang:

Even my new trench coat with fur collar
Ronnie bought for ten cents on the dollar.
Second-hand gowns
And old hand-me-downs,
The china is the only thing that's new!

An admirer of Nancy Reagan, whose identity was not revealed, had tipped her off that mockery of her spending would evoke gales of laughter. Forewarned, she assembled her costume and placed it where she could get into it quickly after slipping unobtrusively from her seat.

Although Nancy's entire ditty would be talked about for years, its punch line referred to a topic that earlier had made front pages throughout the nation.

Admirers showered the Reagans with gifts before they entered the White House, where anything of value would have to be refused. Nancy used a wad of cash, reported to have been more than two hundred thousand dollars to make a special purchase. To the consternation of middle-class America, the first lady blew that bundle on a set of china. Described as being a unique shade of red, each dinner plate had a price tag said to be in excess of one thousand dollars.

Nancy made a record of sorts, but expensive dinnerware for use in the White House was far from new. Generations earlier Elizabeth Monroe startled a then-Puritanical nation. After combing the factories of France, her representatives selected a "state service" for use at diplomatic and other formal dinners. Before closing the deal, agents Russell and Lafarge assured the first lady that no other home in America had china like that selected for her use.

Sparse records do not reveal how many tax dollars went into Elizabeth Monroe's queenly breakables. She seems to have been the first, but far from the last, mistress of the White House who had an unusual interest in china.

Six administrations later, beautiful Sarah Polk tossed her corkscrew curls and announced that she had to have a new set of china. This time the selection was made by W. W. Corcoran, whose name is perpetuated by Washington's Corcoran Gallery of Art.

At the same porcelain plant from which the Monroe china came, Corcoran found what he described as an exquisitely tasteful pattern that managed to be both florid and light. Adorned with small red-white-and-blue eagles and shields, the French-made ware was for a few weeks the talk of Washington.

From 1869 until 1902, the east side of the White House underwent little change, but the dinnerware seemed to change from administration to administration.

In keeping with her New Hampshire background, Jane Pierce wanted little to do with elaborate imported china. She stashed what was left of the Monroe set and most of the Polk set in closets. Soon the first lady triumphantly reported to her husband that she had found "a nice set of American-made blue-and-white dishes" that would be adequate for any occasion.

Mary Todd Lincoln did not go on record with her reaction to blue-and-white for formal dinners. She simply shelved the Pierce dishes and ordered two new sets of Haviland—one for the White House, the other for herself.

Julia Grant, serene in her confidence that no one dared challenge her commitment to the American Union, turned to an import house for something "a bit more eye catching than the blue-and-white."

At J. W. Boeteler & Brother in the capital, she found Haviland porcelain with scalloped edges in a color that she liked. Made to order in France, Julia's six-hundred-piece set featured a gold eagle and shield, a design beginning to be called "the presidential arms." Perhaps as a concession to boosters of America, hand-painted flowers in the centers of her pieces were familiar blossoms rather than exotic European ones.

Lucy Hayes was derided because she served lemonade instead of wine, but when it came to dinnerware she was anything but strait-laced. In the White House conservatory she found ferns that she especially liked. Cuttings of the ferns were shipped to Haviland and Company, where they were copied by artists in the design of her new china.

First used at a banquet in honor of president-elect James A. Garfield and his wife, Lucretia, the Lucy porcelains created a sensation. A few admirers compared the dinner plates with Audubon paintings. Critics scoffed that a person had to turn his eyes away to enjoy eating from a plate on which circling wolves were about to fall upon a buffalo.

The Lucy porcelains featured potatoes, beans, tomatoes, and other vegetables on soup bowls, but the fish plates were adorned with bass, trout, salmon, and shad. Almost inevitably, persimmons, apples, and blueberries adorned the fruit plates.

Few persons who ate from the Lucy porcelains were indifferent. A select handful of connoisseurs agreed that nothing so unusual had ever been seen on an American table. Most people, however, branded them as vulgar and "selected in indescribably bad taste." Helen Taft later relegated what was left of the set to storage bins.

Edith Roosevelt's interest in china caused her to establish a permanent collection of presidential dinnerware at the White House.

Caroline Harrison was a better than passable watercolor artist. By the time she became first lady she had experimented with designing patterns for china. Her hand-painted pieces, always including at least one four-leaf clover, became coveted White House souvenirs.

While inspecting the mansion, Caroline noticed that many shelves were stacked with the remnants of once-notable sets of dinnerware. She sorted out what she considered to be the best pieces and had shelves made on which to display them.

She concluded that the mansion needed yet another new set of china. Inquiries revealed that no American manufacturer then produced porcelain of the quality she wanted. As the slogan "Made in America" was not yet fixed on the national consciousness, she ordered blanks from France. These pieces without patterns were then adorned with two of America's most familiar plants, corn and goldenrod.

About a decade later Edith Roosevelt discovered that Caroline Harrison had stashed away hundreds of chipped and broken pieces not suitable for exhibition. Determined that they would neither be placed on display nor given away as souvenirs, the first lady had the boxes of discarded china destroyed. She then arranged for the Caroline Harrison collection to be displayed more prominently. For use during her tenure, she selected a simple gold-rimmed pattern.

Helen Taft liked the Roosevelt china so much that instead of putting it in storage and ordering a new set, she simply added to what Edith had left behind. Sometimes she went to the display cabinets and selected a few ornate historic pieces to be placed on the table along with the gold-and-white.

When she took over the White House late in 1915, Edith Bolling Galt Wilson went a giant step beyond her predecessors. Thinking that the display shelves were too crowded and too easily overlooked, she created a special China Room close to the newly built Appointment Room. During Bess Truman's tenure, most of the historic china was taken to the White House Museum that features gowns worn by first ladies.

Grace Coolidge and several of her successors were satisfied to keep the Edith Roosevelt pattern in use and to enlarge upon it. Until Lady Bird Johnson came along, few twentieth-century first ladies showed special interest in dinnerware. Although heralded in the press before it hit the tables, her new set decorated with eagles and wild flowers was tame by comparison with what was left of the Lucy Hayes china.

First ladies of the twenty-first century are more likely to spend their time campaigning for their husbands than looking for distinctive dinnerware. Until then, Nancy Reagan's thousand-dollar plates are likely to reign without serious challenge.

38

Abby to the Ark

Nicknames and Terms
of Endearment

As with all families, the first families have used nicknames and other epithets for each other. While most of these are colored with family significance and may date from childhood or were bestowed by family and friends, the political and social aspect has been mined by the press and the public at large whenever the presidential family has fallen under the microscope of scrutiny.

Not counting eight wives who never became mistresses of the White House or the eighteen women who presided over some or many of its functions, first ladies are known by more than a hundred nicknames. Some of them are far more familiar than the owner's baptismal name, but others were forgotten almost as soon as their bearers returned to private life.

Affectionate nicknames, coined by family members or suitors, run the gamut from the ordinary to the unusual. Influenced by the fact that she was the fifth of eight children, Julia Grant was widely known as Little Sister. Another fifth child, Mary Todd Lincoln was called by the same name within her family circle.

John Adams often addressed Abigail as Dear Partner.

Harry Truman simply called his first lady The Boss.

Franklin D. Roosevelt called Eleanor "Babs." This picture is from 1933.

To her children who were adopted by George Washington, Martha was known as Patsy.

Thelma Catherine Ryan, known to posterity as Pat Nixon, was Babe to her father and Buddy to other family members.

To Herbert Hoover, Lou was Mother.

FDR sometimes referred to Eleanor as My Missus or Babs.

Enamored with the novels of Charles Dickens, Eleanor Roosevelt's father borrowed the name of a Dickens character and called his gangling daughter Little Nell.

For reasons never clearly explained, close relatives often used Nina as a tag for young Claudia Alta Taylor—better known as Lady Bird Johnson.

To some relatives and intimates Betty Ford was known as Petunia.

Nancy Reagan occasionally answered to the name of Cuddles.

By far the most persistent endearment bestowed upon a future first lady was Dolley. One of Dorothea Todd's younger brothers tried to master her name but gave up when he only managed to lisp Dolley. His choice stuck so firmly that Dolley Madison is the name known to posterity rather than Dorothea.

Some epithets coined by the press were descriptive rather than affectionate. For Nancy Reagan, it was no compliment to see herself referred to in print as "the First Mannequin."

Frances Folsom, soon to become Mrs. Grover Cleveland, was easily identified when mentioned as "the Bride-Elect."

Bess Truman considered it an honor to be called "the Independent Lady from Independence."

Pat Nixon sometimes glowed when referred to as "the Fair Lady."

For decades everyone who was anyone in Washington knew that a reference to "the Velvet Glove" was a compliment of sorts to Dolley Madison.

Among a handful of intimates Abigail Adams was called "Miss Adorable."

In girlhood Elizabeth Monroe reveled in being known as "the Belle of New York," but Julia Tyler topped her when she was lauded both at home and in Europe as "the Rose of Long Island."

Nursemaid Alice Tittle was so enamored with the child she attended that one day she placed her hands on her hips and exclaimed, "This little girl is as pretty as a Lady Bird!" Little did she know that the whole nation would come to know Claudia Alta Taylor by her nickname when Lyndon Johnson succeeded John F. Kennedy in November 1963.

Lady Bird Johnson was given another nickname when intimates of her rough-and-tumble husband referred to her as Gentle Hand.

*When tiny, her winsomeness caused
the future wife of Lyndon B. Johnson
to be permanently dubbed Lady Bird.*

Equally laudatory, Silver Fox is one of the titles bestowed upon
Barbara Bush.

Georgia native Rosalynn Carter was given the moniker of "the
Steel Magnolia."

To Girl Scouts, whom she once led, Lou Hoover was called Buffalo.

Eleanor Roosevelt's admirers voted her the World's Most Admired
Woman and in print she was known as "the first lady of the world."

Grace Coolidge was designated as "the first lady of Baseball," but
behind her back she was often called "Cal's safety valve."

Admirers of Sarah Polk designated her the president's "guardian."

Mamie Eisenhower was lauded as "the first lady of Femininity,"
but it was Jacqueline Kennedy upon whom the title "queen of
America" was bestowed.

When not termed "Spotless Edie," Florence Harding was often admired as "the Duchess."

Lucy Hayes was "Lemonade Lucy" because of her aversion to serving alcoholic beverages in the White House.

Married to the Father of His Country, it took little imagination to refer to Martha as the Mother of Our Country.

Reporters often wrote of Julia Tyler as "Her Serene Loveliness," but even this title did not quite come up to that of Elizabeth Monroe in Paris where she was lauded as *la belle américaine*.

Betty Ford was called Skipper.

Dolley Madison—Queen Dolley, sometimes—was to capital society "the queen of parties."

Two of the most intriguing nicknames were borrowed from Broadway. Betty Ford was known to some intimates as Pinafore, and from Gilbert and Sullivan's *The Mikado* Frances Cleveland was called Yum-Yum.

Jannetje, a Dutch form of Hannah Van Buren's name, is among the least known of those used by first ladies.

Grover Cleveland persisted in calling Frances Folsom by the name Frank.

Code names adopted by the Secret Service to designate those they guarded may possibly say a bit about a few first ladies. Bess Truman was Fern Lake, and Pat Nixon was Starlight. Dancer referred to Rosalynn Carter, and Barbara Bush was Tranquility.

Not all nicknames were complimentary. Mamie Eisenhower's indifference to politics led some to christen her Sleeping Beauty. Hillary Rodham Clinton, however, had not left Little Rock, Arkansas, before her critics began referring to her as Bill's Boss and The Ark.

Those first ladies without nicknames or colorful monikers are Louisa Adams, Anna Tuthill Harrison, Letitia Christian Tyler, Eliza Johnson, and Ida Saxton McKinley.

39

Florence to Mary Todd

Home Sweet White House

Gay young voices and quick footsteps of grandchildren have enlivened the White House during many administrations. Florence Harding, however, wanted nothing to do with such goings-on. She never invited her two grandchildren to visit her in Washington and seems to have tried to pretend that they did not exist.

Letitia Tyler spent her one year in the White House in a wheel chair after suffering a stroke. Because it was difficult to get the contraption up and down steps, her only appearance during a public ceremony was at the 1842 wedding of her daughter Elizabeth. Distinguished visitors such as Washington Irving and Charles Dickens climbed the stairs to greet her.

Before taking up residence in the mansion, Lucretia Garfield suggested to her husband that elevators be installed, but his assassination after a few months in office postponed the plans.

When Abigail Adams moved into the still-unfinished mansion, she was vexed to discover that the grates in the fireplaces were not suitable for burning coal. To make matters worse, few villagers living nearby were willing to cut wood to the proper length so the place could be heated.

Prowling around used furniture shops in 1901, Edith Roosevelt discovered an antique mahogany sofa and bought it for forty dollars.

Considering it to be just right for the Red Room, she placed her bargain there. When preparing to vacate at the end of her husband's term, she wanted to replace it and take the sofa with her, but some congressmen balked and told her to leave it behind. Her successor, Helen Taft, shipped the sofa to Edith as a New Year's gift in 1910.

During the tenure of Ida McKinley, a clothes closet in the family living quarters was filled with knitting yarn. She said that knitting was her form of relaxation, so she kept her hands busy most waking moments. At least four thousand pairs of slippers for women and children, knitted by the first lady, were given to invalids, charities, and friends.

Grace Coolidge liked to crochet. She started on a bedspread, averaged one square per month, and left the finished piece behind for use on the Lincoln bed.

Eliza Johnson, who was reared as a shoemaker's daughter, very early learned to make-do. She discovered that visitor traffic had reduced some of the White House rugs to tatters. When Congress refused to appropriate funds to replace the worst of them, she showed her daughter Martha how to cover the bare spots with sheets and pillow cases.

Abigail Adams had seldom been sick in her life until she moved into the president's residence in Philadelphia. There she developed severe headaches, caused, it was discovered, by the radical new Argand burners for oil lamps that were installed at the suggestion of scientist-inventor Thomas Jefferson.

Caroline Harrison somewhat doubtfully consented for a new form of energy to be used throughout the White House. As a result, the entire mansion was wired for electricity.

Rosalynn Carter found the place crammed with what she considered entirely too many electrical gadgets. When an inventory showed that the mansion was equipped with 220 FM radios and 325 televisions, she managed to get rid of many of them.

Upon checking the history of the White House, Lou Hoover was dismayed to discover that the chairs used at the signing of the

Rosalynn Carter had superfluous radios and televisions removed from the White House.

Emancipation Proclamation were no longer there. She studied a painting of the signing ceremony, then sent out agents to find the missing chairs. Before her tenure ended, all of them had been restored to the mansion.

Edith Wilson wondered what had happened to some long-familiar accessories. Eventually she discovered two paintings of nudes that Helen Taft had hidden away.

Abigail Adams, who pronounced only six rooms of the mansion to be usable in 1800, decided that the builders had made important omissions. She had a back stairway added—along with a privy. On wash day, the first lady hung clothes to dry in what is now the East Room.

Mamie Eisenhower, noted for regularly inspecting for dust while wearing white gloves, detested anything that seemed to her to be untidy. Many carpets had pile so thick that every footstep made a deep imprint; as a result, she instructed servants and many regular visitors to walk around the edges of rooms.

Francis B. Carpenter's famous painting of the signing of the Emancipation Proclamation shows chairs that were found and restored to the mansion by Lou Hoover.

Nancy Reagan reputedly brought astrologers into the mansion from time to time. Much earlier, the house was used for dabbling in spiritualism. Distraught at the death of her son Willie, Mary Todd Lincoln so desperately wanted to make contact with him that she persuaded the president to attend at least one White House séance.

40

Edith to Lou

Getting Around

*E*xcept for recreational activity, first ladies have seldom mounted a horse. During her eight years as mistress of the White House, Edith Roosevelt frequently lamented the fact that the presidential household did not have one of the new self-propelled vehicles. Her protestations were futile; Teddy stuck to horses, but his was the last administration in which the White House had no automobile.

Martha Washington was often seen in the ornate state coach purchased by the first president. Its cream-colored exterior had gilt frosting and paintings of cherubs and roses. Coachmen, footmen, and outriders were required to wear the orange-and-white livery of Mount Vernon when the huge vehicle lumbered along the streets of the capital, Philadelphia, drawn by six white horses.

Thrifty Abigail Adams persuaded John that he need not go into debt to follow the example of Washington. Thus the first lady and her husband bought a set of secondhand coaches and seven old horses.

Rachel Jackson died before Andrew Jackson assumed office, so she did not get to ride in the splendid coach presented to her husband by the citizens of New York City. Much of the wood for that vehicle was taken from the USS *Constitution,* called Old Ironsides because it was built from the live oaks of the southeastern coast.

Teddy Roosevelt, famous as a "Rough Rider" during the Spanish-American War, preferred horses to cars.

Silver-plated trimmings and crimson satin cushions added to the splendor of the vehicle that the president's wife never saw.

Abigail Fillmore was more fortunate; she was frequently a passenger in a dark green lacquered coach that was trimmed with silver plate. Like Jackson's coach, it was a gift from supporters in New York. The Fillmore coach was finished in blue silk and had window shades and door handles of mother-of-pearl.

At Lucretia Garfield's suggestion, her husband borrowed a coach belonging to Rutherford B. Hayes, which they used during the few months before Garfield was felled by an assassin's bullet.

"No ordinary coach is good enough for my bride," Grover Cleveland announced. Thus the White House acquired a splendid green, black, and pink landau with a roof that could be lowered or even detached.

The small black brougham equipped with glass windows that had been purchased with federal funds in 1902 and used by the

William Howard Taft in one of the many automobiles he purchased for White House use.

Theodore Roosevelts was driven for the last time during inaugural ceremonies for William Howard Taft. Breaking with tradition, the incoming chief executive had the top of the brougham folded back after his inauguration. His wife, Helen, then joined him, becaming the first mistress of the White House to ride to her new home with her husband.

Taft purchased the first White House automobile, a seven-passenger White Steamer. By the time Helen Taft turned the mansion over to Ellen Wilson, four automobiles were garaged there.

In 1915, when the former Edith Bolling Galt became the second Mrs. Woodrow Wilson, the newlyweds rode to the railroad station in a Pierce-Arrow car. Soon after the United States entered World War I, the big auto and its companions were stored on blocks. Edith and Woodrow returned to carriages for their afternoon drives, oblivious to the incongruity of being followed by an auto filled with Secret Service agents.

During Lou Hoover's tenure as mistress of the White House, the lumbering Pierce-Arrow was officially named Car Number One. It remained in use until 1960, when it was replaced by a sixteen-cylinder Cadillac that was supplemented by a fleet of thirteen leased cars.

In the 1990s the White House garage houses stretch limousines and many other autos. No vehicle is called Car Number One, however; that title was dropped when the president's plane, Air Force One, came into use.

Appendix

First Ladies Who Lived into Their Nineties

Bess Truman

First Ladies Who Lived into Their Eighties

Dolley Madison
Anna Harrison
Sarah Polk
Lucretia Garfield
Frances Cleveland

Edith Roosevelt
Helen Taft
Edith Wilson
Mamie Eisenhower

First Ladies Who Were Only Children

Ellen Arthur
Frances Cleveland

Grace Coolidge
Nancy Reagan

First Ladies Whose Birthplaces Are National Historic Sites

Abigail Adams

Mamie Eisenhower

First Ladies Whose Homes Are National Historic Sites

Eleanor Roosevelt

First Ladies Who Were Older Than Their Husbands

Martha Washington
Abigail Fillmore
Caroline Harrison

Florence Harding
Pat Nixon

First Ladies Who Were Widows When They Married

Martha Custis Washington
Dolley Todd Madison

Edith Galt Wilson

First Ladies Who Were Divorcees

Florence DeWolfe Harding

Betty Warren Ford

First Ladies Who Attended the Inauguration of John F. Kennedy

Edith Wilson
Eleanor Roosevelt
Bess Truman
Mamie Eisenhower

Jacqueline Kennedy
Lady Bird Johnson
Pat Nixon
Betty Ford

First Ladies Who Married in Their Teens

Abigail Adams
Elizabeth Monroe
Eliza Johnson

Mamie Eisenhower
Rosalynn Carter

First Ladies Who Had No Children

Sarah Polk

Edith Wilson

Martha Dandridge Custis, one of the wealthiest landowners in Virginia, married twenty-six-year-old Col. George Washington on January 6, 1759, at her estate in New Kent County. The groom wore the dress blue uniform of his regiment, and the bride wore a yellow silk dress with a lace neckline and adorned with pearls. [JUNIUS B. STEARNS PAINTING, LIBRARY OF CONGRESS]

First Ladies Who Married While Their Husbands Were President

Julia Tyler   Edith Wilson
Frances Cleveland

First Ladies Who Had Five or More Children

Abigail Adams   Lucy Hayes
Anna Harrison   Lucretia Garfield
Letitia Tyler   Frances Cleveland
Julia Tyler   Edith Roosevelt
Margaret Taylor   Eleanor Roosevelt
Eliza Johnson   Barbara Bush

This family portrait hung in the Red Room during the eight years Julia Grant was mistress of the mansion. The Grants' only daughter, Ellen, was married to Algernon Charles Frederick Sartoris at the White House in 1874.

First Ladies Who Celebrated Their Golden Wedding Anniversaries

Abigail Adams

Louisa Adams

Bess Truman

Mamie Eisenhower

First Ladies Whose Children Married in the White House

Eliza Monroe

Louisa Adams

Letitia Tyler

Julia Grant

Ellen Wilson

Lady Bird Johnson

Pat Nixon

First Ladies Who Were Graduated from College

Lucy Hayes

Lucretia Garfield

Frances Cleveland

Grace Coolidge

Lou Hoover
Jacqueline Kennedy
Lady Bird Johnson
Pat Nixon

Rosalynn Carter
Nancy Reagan
Hillary Clinton

First Ladies Who Taught School

Abigail Fillmore
Lucretia Garfield
Helen Taft
Ellen Wilson

Lou Hoover
Eleanor Roosevelt
Pat Nixon

First Ladies Awarded Franking Privileges by Congress

Martha Washington
Dolley Madison
Louisa Adams
Anna Harrison
Sarah Polk
Margaret Taylor
Mary Lincoln
Lucretia Garfield
Julia Grant
Frances Cleveland

Ida McKinley
Edith Roosevelt
Edith Wilson
Florence Harding
Eleanor Roosevelt
Bess Truman
Mamie Eisenhower
Jacqueline Kennedy
Lady Bird Johnson

Members of the Daughters of the American Revolution

Julia Dent Grant
Caroline Harrison
  (first president general)
Edith Roosevelt
Florence Harding

Eleanor Roosevelt (resigned)
Mamie Eisenhower
Rosalynn Carter (resigned)
Nancy Reagan
Barbara Bush

First Ladies Who Died in the White House

Letitia Tyler
Caroline Harrison

Ellen Wilson

First Ladies Represented in the Smithsonian Dress Collection

Martha Washington
Abigail Adams
Dolley Madison
Elizabeth Monroe
Louisa Adams
Julia Tyler
Sarah Polk
Abigail Fillmore
Jane Pierce
Mary Lincoln
Julia Grant
Lucy Hayes
Lucretia Garfield
Caroline Harrison
Frances Cleveland
Ida McKinley

Edith Roosevelt
Helen Taft
Ellen Wilson
Edith Wilson
Florence Harding
Grace Coolidge
Lou Hoover
Eleanor Roosevelt
Bess Truman
Mamie Eisenhower
Jacqueline Kennedy
Lady Bird Johnson
Pat Nixon
Betty Ford
Rosalynn Carter
Nancy Reagan

First Ladies Pictured on U.S. Postage Stamps

Martha Washington
Abigail Adams

Dolley Madison
Eleanor Roosevelt

First Ladies Pictured on U.S. Postal Cards

Martha Washington

Index

Boldface entries indicate illustrations